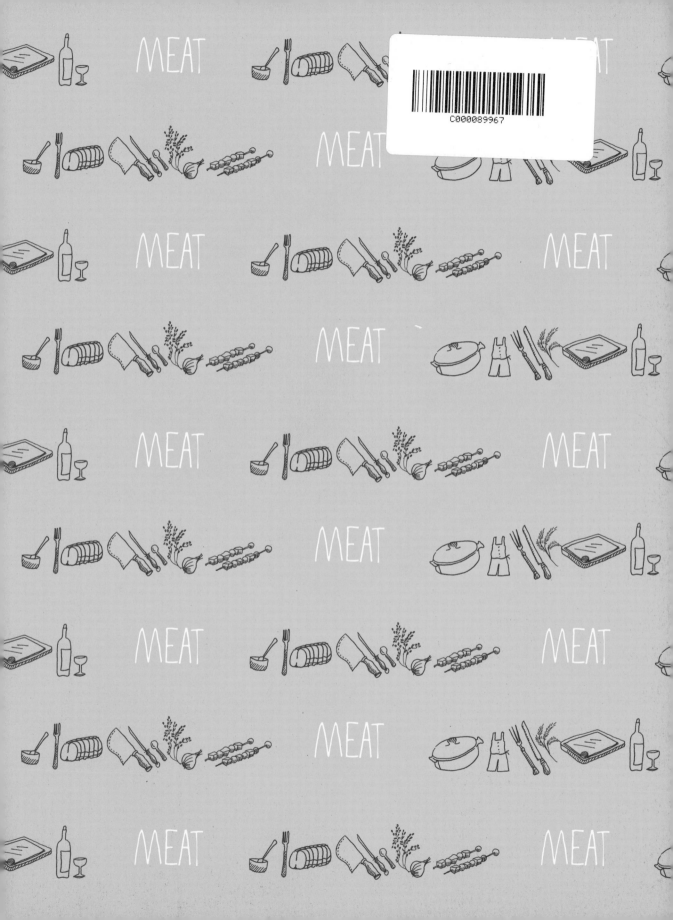

Recipes and food styling by Valéry Drouet
Photography by Pierre-Louis Viel

VALÉRY DROUET & PIERRE-LOUIS VIEL

MEAT

[THE ART OF COOKING MEAT]

h.f.ullmann

BEEF

VEAL

CONTENTS

LAMB

PORK

VARIETY MEATS

SAUCES

CHILI SAUCE

MUSTARD SAUCE

MUSHROOM SAUCE

BÉARNAISE SAUCE

GREEN PEPPERCORN SAUCE

WINE SAUCE

ONION AND CREAM SAUCE

SHALLOT SAUCE

The sauces serve 6. To be eaten with cold meats or grilled meat dishes.

CHILI SAUCE

Peel and chop 2 shallots and 1 garlic clove. Place in a small, high-sided saucepan with ½ cup (120 g) ketchup, ¼ cup (25 g) brown sugar, 3 tablespoons of sweet soy sauce, 1 tablespoon of Tabasco®, ⅔ cup (150 ml) strong veal broth (see recipe on page 12), and salt to taste. Cook for 15 minutes over medium heat, stirring occasionally with a whisk. Blend everything with a hand blender. Serve this sauce hot or cold.

MUSHROOM SAUCE

Clean and thinly slice 14 ounces (400 g) porcini. Pour 2 tablespoons of walnut oil into a saucepan, add 1½ tablespoons of butter, and cook the mushrooms for 5 minutes. Season with salt and pepper and transfer the mushrooms to a plate. Deglaze the saucepan with scant 1 cup (200 ml) strong veal broth over high heat and season with salt and pepper. Reduce the sauce by half over high heat. Pour in ⅔ cup (150 ml) light cream and reduce again until you obtain a fairly thick sauce. Transfer to a high-sided container and blend with a hand blender. Pour the sauce into a saucepan. Add the cooked mushrooms and simmer over low heat for 5 minutes.

MUSTARD SAUCE

Pour ⅔ cup (150 ml) strong veal broth (see recipe on page 12) into a medium-size saucepan, bring to a boil, and cook for 10 minutes. Add ⅔ cup (150 ml) light cream, then season with salt and pepper. Reduce the sauce over medium heat until thick. Add generous 1 tablespoon of strong mustard and 1 tablespoon of wholegrain mustard. Stir the sauce over low heat but do not allow to boil.

BÉARNAISE SAUCE

Melt 1 cup + 2 tablespoons (250 g) of butter in a double boiler, then skim off the foam (the milk proteins) that has formed on the top in order to obtain a clarified butter. Peel and chop 2 ounces (60 g) shallots. Place in a large saucepan with 1 teaspoon of cracked peppercorns, 1 tablespoon of chopped tarragon, and ⅔ cup (150 ml) white vinegar. Reduce over medium heat until the liquid has evaporated. Add 4 egg yolks and 2 tablespoons of cold water; whisk for 6–8 minutes over low heat until smooth. Gradually whisk in the clarified butter; season with salt and pepper. Strain the béarnaise sauce, then add 1 tablespoon of chopped tarragon.

GREEN PEPPERCORN SAUCE

Dry-fry 2 tablespoons of green peppercorns in a saucepan. Pour in 3 tablespoons of brandy, flambé, and reduce over medium heat. Pour in 3 tablespoons of port and reduce slightly once again. Pour in scant 1 cup strong veal broth (see recipe on page 12), season with salt, and reduce for 10 minutes over medium heat. Stir in generous 2 tablespoons of thick sour cream or crème fraîche and boil over high heat for 5 minutes, whisking constantly to make a fairly thick sauce. Blend the sauce with a hand blender.

ONION AND CREAM SAUCE

Peel and chop 1 large onion, then put in a saucepan with Ð cup (150 ml) white vinegar. Cook, uncovered, over medium heat until nearly all the liquid has evaporated. Pour in 1¼ cups (300 ml) light sour cream or crème fraîche; season to taste. Reduce the sauce by half over medium heat until thick, whisking occasionally.

WINE SAUCE

Peel and chop 5 ounces (150 g) shallots. Put the chopped shallots in a saucepan with 1¾ cups (400 ml) red wine and 1 sprig thyme. Reduce by two-thirds over medium heat. Pour in scant 1 cup (200 ml) strong veal broth (see recipe on page 12); season with salt and pepper. Reduce for 15 minutes over medium heat until smooth. At the end of the cooking time, whisk in 1½ tablespoons (20 g) of butter.

SHALLOT SAUCE

Peel and thinly slice 14 ounces (400 g) shallots. Cook the shallots in $^1/_3$ cup (80 g) butter in a wide saucepan for 30 minutes over low heat, stirring occasionally. Season with salt and pepper. Pour in generous 1 cup (250 ml) strong veal broth (see recipe on page 12) and simmer for 15–20 minutes.

BROTHS

PREPARATION: **30 minutes**
COOKING TIME: **4 hours 30 minutes**
REFRIGERATION: **overnight**

STRONG VEAL BROTH

≫ The day before, roast 4½ pounds (2 kg) veal bones, chopped into pieces, in the oven, pre-heated to 400 °F (200 °C), and 5 ounces (150 g) chopped veal shoulder or shank in a roasting pan for 30–40 minutes.

≫ Dry-fry 2 onions, peeled and cut in half (cut-side down), in a skillet for a few minutes over high heat until very well browned.

≫ Peel and trim 5 ounces (150 g) carrots, 3½ ounces (100 g) celery, and 3½ ounces (100 g) leek (white part only). Chop finely.

≫ Put the bones and the roasted meat in a large saucepan. Skim off the fat from the roasting pan and deglaze it with 1 large glass of water. Pour the resulting liquid into the saucepan, add the vegetables, the halved onions, ½ calf's foot, and 1 bouquet garni. Cook for 5 minutes over high heat to brown well. Pour in enough cold water to cover. Bring to a boil and cook, uncovered, for at least 4 hours on a gentle boil, skimming the surface frequently. Strain the broth and cool. Chill overnight in the refrigerator.

≫ The following day, remove and discard the layer of fat which has formed on the surface. Pour the liquid into a large saucepan and reduce it by about half to obtain a strong veal broth.

LAMB BROTH

≫ The day before, place 4½ pounds (2 kg) lamb bones, chopped into pieces, and 2 onions, peeled and cut in half, in a roasting pan for 30 minutes to brown lightly in the oven, pre-heated to 400 °F (200 °C).

≫ Peel, trim, and thinly slice 7 ounces (200 g) carrots and celery.

≫ Put the roasted lamb bones and onions in a large saucepan.

≫ Skim off the fat from the roasting pan and deglaze it with 1 large glass of water. Pour the liquid into the saucepan, add 1 tablespoon of tomato paste, 4 tomatoes, cut in half, the carrots, and the celery. Cook for 5 minutes over high heat, stirring when necessary. Brown for 5 minutes over high heat. Pour in enough cold water to cover and add 1 bouquet garni. Bring to a boil and cook, uncovered, for at least 4 hours on a gentle boil, skimming the surface regularly.

≫ Strain the broth and cool. Chill overnight in the refrigerator.

≫The following day, remove and discard the layer of fat which has formed on the top. Pour the liquid into a large saucepan and reduce it by about half to obtain a strong lamb broth.

STEAK AU POIVRE—THE REAL THING

PREPARATION: **30 minutes**
COOKING TIME: **25 minutes**

INGREDIENTS

Serves 6

- 6 rump steaks weighing approx.
  7 oz (200 g) (or other prime-cut
  steaks)
- 3¼ lb (1.5 kg) potatoes, suitable
  for making fries
- oil for frying
- 3 oz (80 g) cracked peppercorns
- 3 tbsp vegetable oil
- ²/₃ cup (150 ml) brandy
- generous ¾ cup (200 ml) port
- 1¼ cups (300 ml) strong veal
  broth (see recipe on page 12)
- 2 tbsp thick sour cream or crème
  fraîche
- salt, freshly ground pepper

≫ Peel the potatoes and cut them into large fries. Wash them and dry with a clean kitchen cloth.

≫ Heat the frying oil to 300 °F (150 °C). Drop the fries into the hot oil and deep-fry for 5 minutes, then drain them. Cool.

≫ Sprinkle the cracked peppercorns over the steaks, pressing down lightly so they stick to the meat.

≫ Heat 3 tablespoons of oil in a skillet and cook the steaks for 3–8 minutes on each side, depending on whether you like your meat rare, medium, or well done. Transfer the steaks to a plate and put another plate on top to keep them warm.

≫ Skim the fat from the skillet and heat it over high heat. Pour in the brandy, flambé it, and reduce by two-thirds. Add the port and reduce this also by two-thirds so the sauce is syrupy. Pour in the broth and reduce by half. Whisk in the sour cream. Check the seasoning. Put the steaks in the sauce and reheat them for 3–4 minutes.

≫ Meanwhile, increase the temperature of the deep-fryer to 355 °F (180 °C), then cook the fries in hot oil once again until crisp and golden. Drain and season with salt. Serve immediately with the steaks au poivre.

LACQUERED FILLET STEAK WITH DEEP-FRIED ONIONS

PREPARATION: **30 minutes**
MARINADE: **24 hours**
COOKING TIME: **15 minutes**

INGREDIENTS

Serves 6

- 2 lb (900 g) fillet steak
- 3½ oz (100 g) ginger
- 3 tbsp vegetable oil
- generous ¾ cup (200 ml) sweet soy sauce
- scant 1 tsp sweet paprika
- 1 bunch small onions or scallions
- 1 quart (1 liter) oil for frying
- 5 oz (150 g) mesclun salad
- 1 bunch chives, cut into short lengths
- 1 bunch chervil
- 2 tbsp sherry vinegar
- 3 tbsp olive oil
- salt, freshly ground pepper

≫ The day before, peel and chop the ginger. Cut the beef fillet into two lengthways and heat the vegetable oil in a skillet. Cook the beef over high heat for 3–4 minutes to seal all over. Transfer to a plate. Skim the fat from the skillet then deglaze with generous ¾ cup (200 ml) sweet soy sauce. Add the chopped ginger and the sweet paprika. Season generously with pepper and add salt. Reduce until syrupy.

≫ Put the beef pieces back into the skillet and coat with sauce. Cook for 3–4 minutes over high heat so the surface of the beef becomes "lacquered" in appearance (it should remain rare inside). Place on a rack and cool. Wrap tightly in plastic wrap. Chill for 24 hours in the refrigerator.

≫ The next day, peel the onions, leaving a bit of green stalk attached to their bulbs. Heat the oil for deep-frying to about 355 °F (180 °C) and fry the onions for 5–6 minutes. Drain on absorbent paper towels and season with salt.

≫ Wash the mesclun and the herbs. Mix the sherry vinegar and the olive oil in a salad bowl and season with salt and pepper. Add the mesclun, chives, and chervil.

≫ Take the beef out of the refrigerator, discard the plastic wrap, and cut it into slices ¼–½ in (8–10 mm) thick. Arrange on plates with the onions and pour over a little soy sauce. Serve with the salad.

RIB OF BEEF WITH BURGUNDY SAUCE

PREPARATION: **50 minutes**
COOKING TIME: **1¹/₂ hours**
STANDING TIME: **10 minutes**

INGREDIENTS

Serves 6

- 2 rib steaks weighing about 1½ lb (700 g) each
- 6 large floury potatoes
- 6 small sprigs thyme
- 4 shallots, peeled and chopped
- 2½ cups (600 ml) Burgundy (or other full-bodied good red wine)
- 1 tbsp superfine sugar
- generous 1 cup (250 ml) veal broth
- 7 oz (200 g) black grapes, washed
- 7 oz (200 g) Époisses cheese (unpasteurized cow's milk cheese)
- generous 1 tbsp thick sour cream
- 3 tbsp grapeseed oil
- salt, freshly ground pepper

》 Pre-heat the oven to 355 °F (180 °C). Wash the potatoes but leave them unpeeled. Cut 6 pieces of aluminum foil and place 1 sprig of thyme and 1 potato in each. Season with salt and pepper. Wrap the potatoes in the foil and place in an ovenproof dish. Bake in the oven for 45 minutes.

》 Meanwhile, put the shallots in a large saucepan with the wine and sugar. Season with salt and pepper. Reduce the mixture by two-thirds over medium heat. Pour in the veal broth and reduce again, to obtain a smooth sauce. At the end of the cooking time, add the washed grapes. Keep this sauce hot in a double boiler.

》 Take the potatoes out of the oven, and leave them to cool a little. Discard the aluminum foil, cut a lid in the potatoes, and carefully scoop out the filling. Reserve the potato skins. Put the potato filling in a bowl with half the Époisses cheese, cut into small pieces, and the sour cream. Season with salt and pepper. Spoon this mixture into the potato skins and place them in an ovenproof dish. Slice the remaining Époisses cheese and use to cover the tops of the potatoes.

》 Heat the grapeseed oil in a skillet and brown the ribs of beef for 2 minutes on each side before placing on a baking tray. Cook in the oven for 10–15 minutes, depending on whether you like your meat rare, medium, or well done. Take the beef out of the oven and rest it for 10 minutes wrapped in aluminum foil.

》 Meanwhile, place the potatoes under the broiler to reheat and brown. Thinly slice the meat and serve with the stuffed potatoes and the Burgundy sauce.

CHUCK STEAK WITH MUSTARD SAUCE

PREPARATION: 30 minutes
CHILLING TIME: overnight
COOKING TIME: 3 hours

INGREDIENTS

Serves 6

- 2 lb (900 g) chuck under blade steak in one piece
- 1 carrot
- 1 leek, white part only
- 1 bunch celery
- 1 onion
- 2 cloves
- 1 bouquet garni
- 1 head frisée salad
- 1 bunch red spring onions
- generous 2 tbsp strong mustard
- 1 anchovy fillet, preserved in oil
- 3 tbsp aged wine vinegar
- ½ cup (100 ml) olive oil
- salt, freshly ground pepper

⟩ The day before, peel and trim the carrot, leek, celery, and onion, studding the onion with the cloves. Truss up the piece of beef with twine as you would a roast and place it in a large saucepan. Cover with cold water and bring to a boil. Discard the water, drain the rolled meat, and put it back into the cleaned-out saucepan. Add the carrot, onion, celery, leek, and the bouquet garni. Season with salt and pepper. Pour in enough cold water to cover, bring to a boil, and cook, covered, for 3 hours over low heat, skimming the surface regularly. Take off the heat and cool the chuck steak in the saucepan.

⟩ Drain the meat and reserve ½ cup (100 ml) of the cooking liquid. Wrap it tightly in several layers of plastic wrap. Put the meat and reserved cooking broth in the refrigerator to chill overnight.

⟩ The next day, wash the salad. Peel and thinly slice the red onions. Take the meat out of the refrigerator, discard the plastic wrap, and thinly slice the rolled steak. Discard the twine. Strain the reserved broth.

⟩ Put the mustard in a high-sided container and add the anchovy fillet, vinegar, olive oil, and strained broth. Season with salt and pepper. Blend with a hand blender until you have a smooth salad dressing.

⟩ Divide the salad, red onions, and the chuck steak slices among 6 plates or bowls then add a generous amount of salad dressing to each. (Sprinkle with a few golden croutons fried in oil if desired.)

BEEF FILLET WITH PORT

PREPARATION: **35 minutes**
COOKING TIME: **45 minutes**
STANDING TIME: **15 minutes**

INGREDIENTS

Serves 6

- 3 lb 11 oz (1.2 kg) beef fillet in one piece
- 3¼ lb (1.5 kg) floury potatoes
- 3½ oz (100 g) capers in vinegar
- 3 tbsp grapeseed oil
- 1¼ cups (300 ml) milk
- generous 4 tbsp thick sour cream
- 13 tbsp (180 g) butter
- 14 oz (400 g) button mushrooms
- 1¼ cups (300 ml) port
- generous 1 cup (250 ml) veal broth
- salt, freshly ground pepper

≫ Pre-heat the oven to 400 °F (200 ° C).

≫ Peel the potatoes and cut them into large pieces. Cook for 20 minutes in a saucepan filled with salted water.

≫ Drain the capers and chop. Heat the milk in a saucepan.

≫ Drain the potatoes and mash through a ricer, add the hot milk, 3 tablespoons sour cream, 9 tablespoons of butter (130 g), cut into pieces, and the capers. Season with salt and pepper. Keep the mashed potatoes warm in a bain-marie.

≫ Place the meat in an ovenproof dish. Pour over grapeseed oil and dot with 1½ tablespoons (20 g)of diced butter; season with salt and pepper. Cook in the oven for 10 minutes then lower the temperature to 355 °F (180 °C) and cook for a further 10—15 minutes.

≫ Meanwhile, wash and thinly slice the mushrooms. Heat the remaining butter in a skillet and cook the mushrooms for 5—7 minutes. Season with salt and pepper then transfer to a plate. Deglaze the skillet with the port and reduce by two-thirds. Pour in the veal broth, season with salt and pepper, and reduce by half. Add the remaining sour cream, bring to a boil, and cook for 3 minutes over high heat, whisking constantly. Add the mushrooms to the sauce and keep warm.

≫ Take the meat out of the oven, wrap in aluminum foil, and rest for 15 minutes. Thinly slice the meat and serve immediately with the caper-flavored mashed potatoes and the mushroom sauce.

Ginger and soy lacquered beef steak

PREPARATION: **40 minutes**
COOKING TIME: **30 minutes**

INGREDIENTS

Serves 6
- 2¼ lb (1 kg) top or bottom round
  of beef, cut into strips
- 2 large leeks, white part only
- 3 lb 11 oz (1.2 kg) sweet potatoes
- 2½ tbsp (40 g) butter
- 1¾ oz (50 g) ginger
- 3 cloves garlic
- 3 tbsp all-purpose flour
- 1 quart (1 liter) oil for frying
- 3 tbsp grapeseed oil
- ⅔ cup (150 ml) sweet soy sauce
- 7 tbsp (100 ml) salty soy sauce
- salt, freshly ground pepper

≫ Pre-heat the oven to 355 °F (180 °C).

≫ Wash the white part of the leeks and cut into thin strips. Peel the sweet potatoes and cut them into 4 x ⅓-inch- (10 × 1-cm-) strips.

≫ Melt the butter in a saucepan over low heat.

≫ Put the sweet potato strips on a baking tray lined with siliconized paper. Brush them with melted butter and season with salt and pepper. Bake in the oven for 20 minutes.

≫ Meanwhile, peel and chop the ginger and garlic cloves. Put the leek strips in a bowl and stir in the flour.

≫ Heat the oil for frying to about 355 °F (180 °C) in a deep-fryer or large saucepan and then deep-fry the leek strips for a few minutes, until crisp and lightly browned. Drain on absorbent paper towels; season with salt.

≫ Heat the grapeseed oil in a large skillet and brown the meat pieces for 2 minutes over high heat. Transfer to a plate.

≫ Brown the ginger and garlic in the skillet for 2 minutes. Deglaze the skillet with both types of soy sauce. Season with pepper and reduce until thickened.

≫ Put the meat pieces back in the skillet and heat for 3 minutes, coating well with sauce to lacquer them. Serve immediately with the sweet potato and the deep-fried leek strips.

COTTAGE PIE

INGREDIENTS

Serves 6
- 2 lb (900 g) leftover cooked beef
- 2¼ lb (1 kg) floury potatoes
- 10 large shallots
- 3½ oz (100 g) breadcrumbs
- ⅔ cup (150 ml) milk
- ⅔ cup (150 ml) veal broth
- ⅔ cup (150 ml) white wine
- 2 tbsp thick sour cream
- 13 tbsp (180 g) butter
- salt, freshly ground pepper

》 Trim and thinly slice the shallots. Heat 2 tablespoons (30 g) of butter in a saucepan and cook the shallots for 10 minutes over low heat.

》 Break up the meat with your hands or fine chop it with a knife. Put it in the saucepan with the shallots. Pour over the white wine, bring to a boil, and cook for 3 minutes. Add the veal broth and season with salt and pepper. Simmer for 20 minutes over medium heat.

》 Meanwhile, peel the potatoes and cut them into pieces. Cook for 20 minutes in a saucepan filled with salted water.

》 Pre-heat the oven to 400 °F (200 °C).

》 Heat the milk. Drain the potatoes and mash through a ricer. Add generous 7 tablespoons (100 g) of butter, the warm milk, and sour cream. Season with salt and pepper. Stir until smooth.

》 Grease an ovenproof dish with butter. Put the meat at the bottom and cover with mashed potatoes. Sprinkle breadcrumbs over the top and dot with finely diced butter.

》 Bake in the oven for 25—30 minutes. Serve immediately.

Broiled chuck steak with rosemary

PREPARATION: **30 minutes**
REFRIGERATION: **overnight**
COOKING TIME: **30 minutes**
STANDING TIME: **10 minutes**

INGREDIENTS

Serves 6

- 2 chuck under blade steaks weighing about 2 lb (900 g) each
- 2 large sprigs rosemary
- 3 large shallots, peeled and chopped
- generous 1 tsp cracked peppercorns
- 2 sprigs tarragon, leaves only, chopped
- 7 tbsp (100 ml) white wine vinegar
- 3 large tomatoes
- 1 cup + 2 tbsp (250g) butter
- 4 egg yolks
- salt, freshly ground pepper

≫ The day before, crush the rosemary sprigs coarsely in a small mincer. Mix them in a bowl with a little ground pepper. Sprinkle the mixture over the meat, coating all sides and pressing down well. Wrap tightly in plastic wrap and chill overnight in the refrigerator.

≫ The next day, put the shallots in a large saucepan and add the cracked peppercorns, half the tarragon, and the vinegar. Reduce this mixture over medium heat until nearly all the liquid has evaporated, and allow to cool.

≫ Plunge the tomatoes for 20 seconds in a saucepan filled with boiling water. Drain, skin and de-seed, then crush them. Put them in a large saucepan and cook for 10 minutes over low heat. Process with a hand blender for a smooth consistency.

≫ Melt the butter in a double boiler then clarify it (remove the milk proteins). Put the egg yolks in the saucepan in which you have reduced the shallot mixture. Pour in a little cold water and whisk vigorously for 6–8 minutes over low heat to obtain a smooth sauce. Away from the heat, gradually whisk in the clarified butter. Strain the sauce. Stir it into the tomato mixture, adding the remaining tarragon. Reserve this 'Choron' sauce.

≫ Take the beef out of the refrigerator, discard the plastic wrap, and broil the meat under a very hot broiler or on a grill for 8–15 minutes on each side, depending on whether you like your meat rare, medium, or well done. Season with salt. Cover with aluminum foil and rest for 10 minutes.

≫ Cut the meat into thin slices and serve with the Choron sauce. Accompany with small sautéed potatoes.

BEEF AND TARRAGON TERRINE

PREPARATION: 45 minutes
REFRIGERATION: overnight
COOKING TIME: 30 minutes
(for the carrots)

INGREDIENTS

Serves 6
- 2 lb (900 g) assorted cooked (boiled) beef cuts left over from a pot-au-feu
- 3 carrots
- 2 leaves gelatin
- 4 sprigs tarragon
- 1½ quarts (1.5 liters) beef broth from a pot-au-feu
- 3 tbsp tarragon vinegar
- generous 1 tbsp strong mustard
- 7 tbsp (100 ml) vegetable oil
- salt, freshly ground pepper

⟩ The day before, peel the carrots and keep them whole.

⟩ Soak the gelatin leaves for 10 minutes in cold water. Take the leaves off the sprig of tarragon and chop.

⟩ Bring the broth to a boil in a large saucepan. Add the carrots and cook for 30 minutes. Cut into pieces.

⟩ Strain $1^2/_3$ cups (400 ml) broth and pour into a large saucepan. Reduce by a third. Away from the heat, add the drained and squeezed gelatin leaves to the saucepan and half the chopped tarragon leaves.

⟩ Line a terrine dish with plastic wrap. Chop the meat into small pieces. Pour a little tarragon-flavored beef broth in the terrine dish. Line the bottom of the terrine with half the beef pieces, pour a little more broth over them, and cover with a layer of carrot pieces. Pour in more broth then arrange the remaining pieces of beef in another layer. Pour in the remaining broth. Chill the terrine overnight in the refrigerator.

⟩ The next day, shortly before serving the terrine, stir the vinegar, mustard, oil, and the remaining tarragon in a bowl. Season with salt and pepper. Whisk until emulsified to a smooth dressing.

⟩ Place the bottom of the terrine dish under running hot water and carefully remove the terrine from the mold. Slice and serve with the dressing.

CHUCK STEAK IN WINE

PREPARATION: **30 minutes**
COOKING TIME: **3¼ hours**

INGREDIENTS

Serves 6

- 6 chuck under blade steaks weighing about 7½ oz (220 g) each
- 2 onions
- 3 cloves garlic
- 1 stick celery
- 1 large carrot
- 3 tbsp vegetable oil
- 1 quart (1 liter) red wine
- 2 cups (500 ml) veal broth
- 2 sprigs thyme
- 3¼ cups (750 ml) milk
- 3 tbsp olive oil
- 3½ tbsp (50 g) butter, cut into small pieces
- 3½ oz (100 g) dried tomatoes, chopped
- 5½ oz (150 g) polenta
- salt, freshly ground pepper

》Trim and peel the onions, 2 garlic cloves, the celery stick and the carrot, and cut them all into small dice.

》Heat the vegetable oil in a very large saucepan and seal the chuck steaks on both sides over high heat. Transfer the meat to a plate. Put the diced vegetables in the saucepan, and cook for 5 minutes over medium heat.

》Pour the wine into the saucepan and bring to a boil. Put the chuck steaks in the saucepan and add the veal broth and thyme. Season with salt and pepper. Simmer, covered, for 3 hours over low heat, turning the meat frequently and skimming the surface.

》Place the cooked steaks on a plate and cover with aluminum foil. Reduce the cooking liquid until syrupy, then strain.

》Clean the saucepan and pour in the strained sauce. Add the steaks and keep hot.

》Put the milk, olive oil, and the last whole peeled garlic clove in another saucepan. Season with salt and pepper and bring to a boil. Add the polenta, sprinkling it into the milk while stirring. Lower the heat and cook for 6–8 minutes, stirring constantly.

》Away from the heat, stir in the butter and the finely chopped dried tomatoes. Mix well. Serve this polenta with the beef.

BOEUF BOURGUIGNON

PREPARATION: **30 minutes**
COOKING TIME: **2¼ hours**

INGREDIENTS

Serves 6
- 3½ lb (1.6 kg) beef chuck roast or round roast, cut into large pieces
- 1 large yellow onion
- 1 carrot
- 3 tbsp vegetable oil
- 7 tbsp (60 g) all-purpose flour
- 1 quart (1 liter) red wine
- 2 cups (500 ml) veal broth
- 2 sprigs thyme
- 1 bay leaf
- 1¼ lb (800 g) white button mushrooms
- ⅓ cup (80 g) butter
- pearl onions
- 3 slices bacon, ½ in (8–10 mm) thick
- salt, freshly ground pepper

≫ Peel and thinly slice the onion and carrot.

≫ Heat the oil in a very large saucepan and seal the meat on all sides over high heat. Add the onion and cook for 3 minutes. Sprinkle with the flour and season with salt and pepper. Cook for 3 minutes over a high heat, turning the meat to coat all over with the flour and oil mixture.

≫ Pour the wine into the saucepan, bring to a boil, and cook for 5 minutes. Add the veal broth, carrot, thyme, and bay leaf. Cook, covered, for 1 hour 30 minutes over low heat, skimming the surface regularly.

≫ Meanwhile, clean the mushrooms and cut each into four. Heat 2½ tablespoons (40 g) of butter in a skillet and cook them for 10 minutes. Season with salt and pepper.

≫ Heat the remaining butter in a large saucepan and cook the peeled pearl onions for 5 minutes. Pour in enough water to cover. Lay a sheet of siliconized paper on top and cook for 10 minutes over medium heat.

≫ Cut the bacon into strips and dry-fry these in a skillet for 5 minutes over high heat.

≫ After the meat has been cooking for 1 hour 30 minutes, check the seasoning then add the small onions, bacon strips, and the mushrooms. Cover and cook for a further 45 minutes over low heat, stirring frequently. Serve the Boeuf bourguignon very hot with steamed potatoes.

POT-AU-FEU WITH THAI BROTH

PREPARATION: **30 minutes**
COOKING TIME: **3½ hours**

INGREDIENTS

Serves 6

- generous 4 lb (1.8 kg) assorted beef cuts (blade portion of beef chuck, beef short ribs, rump pot roast, heel of round)
- 4 carrots
- 12 small turnips
- 4 small leeks
- 2 onions
- 2 stalks lemon grass
- 10 black peppercorns
- 2 marrowbones
- 1 large bouquet garni
- 1 small Savoy cabbage
- 7 tbsp (100 ml) soy sauce
- ½ red chile
- 12 leaves Thai or regular basil
- salt

To serve

- sea salt, horseradish

》 Tightly truss up each beef cut separately.

》 Peel the carrots, turnips, leeks, and onions; keep them whole. Discard the outer leaves of the lemon grass stalks and thinly slice the tender, inner part.

》 Put the meat in a very large saucepan and cover with cold water. Bring to a boil, skimming the surface, then drain (discard the water). Clean out the saucepan, put the meat back in it, and completely cover with cold water. Season with salt and add the peppercorns, the marrowbones wrapped in cheesecloth, and the bouquet garni. Bring to a boil. Cover the saucepan and cook for 1 hour over low heat.

》 Put the carrots, leeks, turnips, onions, and three-quarters of the lemon grass in the saucepan. Cook for a further 1 hour 30 minutes over low heat.

》 Cut the cabbage into large pieces. Add to the saucepan and cook for 1 hour.

》 At the end of the cooking time, strain 1 quart (1 liter) of the broth and pour it into another saucepan. Add the soy sauce and the remaining lemon grass. Bring to a boil and cook for 5 minutes.

》 De-seed the chile and chop it. Snip the basil into small pieces with scissors.

》 Take the meat out of the broth and cut it into pieces. Put an equal amount of chopped chile and basil at the bottom of 6 deep plates. Lay the meat pieces and vegetables on top then cover with very hot soy-flavored broth. Serve immediately, with sea salt and horseradish on the side.

PREPARATION: **45 minutes**
COOKING TIME: **50 minutes**

ENTRECÔTE STEAKS WITH BURGUNDY SAUCE

INGREDIENTS

Serves 6

- 6 thick entrecôte steaks weighing about 7½–9 oz (220–250 g) each
- 4 cloves garlic
- 2¼ lb (1 kg) potatoes
- 1 ⅔ cups (400 ml) milk
- 1¼ cups (300 ml) light cream
- 2 large pinches nutmeg
- 8 shallots
- 3¼ cups (750 ml) Burgundy (or other full-bodied good red wine)
- ⅔ cup (150 ml) strong veal broth (see recipe on page 12)
- 2 tbsp (30 g) butter, chilled
- salt, freshly ground pepper

》 Peel and chop the garlic cloves. Peel the potatoes and slice them into rounds approximately ¼ inch (3–4 mm) thick. Put the potato slices in a large saucepan. Pour in the milk and the light cream, and add the garlic cloves and nutmeg. Season with salt and pepper. Bring slowly to a boil and cook for 20 minutes over medium heat, stirring frequently.

》 Meanwhile, peel and chop the shallots. Put them in another saucepan and pour in the red wine. Bring to a boil and reduce by three-quarters.

》 Pre-heat the oven to 355 °F (180 °C).

》 Drain the potatoes, reserving the cooking liquid, and put them in a single large gratin dish or in individual heatproof dishes with a little of the liquid. Make the surface level. Bake in the oven for 20–30 minutes to brown well on top.

》 Pour the veal broth into the saucepan containing the shallots and wine and cook for a further 10 minutes until the sauce has reduced and thickened slightly. Whisk in chilled butter, cut into small pieces. Keep hot in a double boiler.

》 Grill the entrecôte steaks on a barbecue or broil in a cast-iron broiling pan for 3–6 minutes on each side, depending on whether you like your meat rare, medium, or well done. Season with salt and pepper. Serve immediately with the Burgundy sauce and the hot Dauphinoise potatoes.

CARBONNADE OF BEEF

PREPARATION: **30 minutes**
COOKING TIME: **3¼ hours**

INGREDIENTS

Serves 6

- 3½ lb (1.6 kg) beef chuck eye roast, cut into 6 thick slices
- 2 yellow onions
- 3 slices honey spice bread (pain d'épices)
- 3 tbsp strong mustard
- 3 tbsp grapeseed oil
- 2 tbsp (30 g) butter
- 9 tbsp (120 g) brown sugar
- 3 cups (700 ml) dark strong ale (Belgian type)
- 1 ²/₃ cups (400 ml) veal broth
- salt, freshly ground pepper

≫ Pre-heat the oven to 285 °F (140 °C).

≫ Peel and thinly slice the onions. Remove the crusts from the honey spice bread slices then spread with mustard.

≫ Heat the oil in a very large flameproof casserole dish and seal the meat on all sides over high heat. Transfer to a plate.

≫ Put the butter in the casserole dish. Add the onions and cook for 10 minutes over medium heat until extremely tender.

≫ Sprinkle the onions with the sugar and caramelize slightly. Put the meat pieces back in the dish. Pour in the beer and bring to a boil. Add the veal broth and season with salt and pepper. Lay the spice bread slices spread with mustard on top.

≫ Cover the dish and place in the oven. Cook for 3 hours, stirring very carefully without disturbing the spice bread topping after 2 hours' cooking time and not before.

≫ Serve the Carbonnade with homemade fries.

TIP

For a Carbonnade that melts in the mouth and requires only 2 hours 30 minutes' cooking time, use beef flank steak instead of chuck eye roast.

BEEF FILLET WITH HORN OF PLENTY MUSHROOMS

PREPARATION: **30 minutes**
COOKING TIME: **30 minutes**

INGREDIENTS

Serves 6
- 6 slices beef fillet weighing
  6½–7 oz (180–200 g) each
- 1¾ lb (800 g) fresh horn of plenty
  mushrooms
- 3 bay leaves
- 2 shallots
- 2 cups (500 ml) veal broth
- 6 tbsp (90 g) butter, chilled
- 3 tbsp vegetable oil
- salt, freshly ground pepper

》 Pour the veal broth into a large saucepan, add the bay leaves, season with salt and pepper, and reduce by half over medium heat.

》 Meanwhile, rinse the horn of plenty mushrooms briefly under a trickle of cold running water.

》 Peel and chop the shallots. Melt 2 tablespoons (30 g) of butter in a skillet and cook the shallots for 4–5 minutes over gentle heat. Increase the heat and immediately tip the mushrooms into the skillet. Braise them for 5–6 minutes, stirring constantly, and drain in a conical sieve, reserving the cooking liquid. Pour the liquid into the saucepan containing the veal broth.

》 When the veal broth has reduced, whisk in the remaining butter, cut into small pieces, over high heat. Discard the bay leaves. Blend the sauce with a hand blender.

》 Heat the vegetable oil in a large skillet and fry the fillet slices for 3–8 minutes on each side, depending on whether you like your meat rare, medium, or well done. Transfer to a plate. Skim the oil from the skillet and heat the mushrooms in the meat juices for 2 minutes.

》 Pour the sauce into the skillet, stirring constantly, then put the fillet slices back in. Simmer for 3–4 minutes over low heat. Serve immediately.

VEAL ROAST WITH JUNIPER BERRIES

PREPARATION: 30 minutes
MARINADE: 24 hours
COOKING TIME: 50 minutes
STANDING TIME: 15 minutes

INGREDIENTS

Serves 6

- 1 piece veal tenderloin weighing about 2¾ lb (1.2 kg)
- 25 juniper berries
- 2 small bunches young carrots, leaves attached
- 7 tbsp (100 ml) olive oil
- $^1/_3$ cup (80 ml) gin
- generous ¾ cup (200 ml) veal broth
- 2 tbsp (30 g) butter, chilled
- salt, freshly ground pepper

≫ The day before, chop the juniper berries with a knife. Spread over the veal roast and wrap tightly in plastic wrap. Chill in the refrigerator for 24 hours.

≫ The next day, pre-heat the oven to 355 °F (180 °C).

≫ Peel and trim the carrots, leaving about ½ inch of green stalk (about 1 cm) attached to them. Put in an ovenproof dish and pour over half of the olive oil. Season with salt and pepper.

≫ Remove the plastic wrap from the meat. Put the veal roast in a flameproof dish. Season with salt and pepper, and pour over the remaining oil. Cook in the oven for 35—40 minutes.

≫ At the same time, cook the carrots on the bottom shelf of the oven for 30 minutes, turning them frequently.

≫ Take the roast out of the oven, wrap in aluminum foil, and allow to rest for 15 minutes.

≫ Skim the oil off the surface of the liquid left in the dish. Place the dish on a medium heat and deglaze it with the gin. Increase the heat and reduce slightly. Add the veal broth, season with salt and pepper, and reduce again, by half. Whisk in the butter. Strain the sauce and keep warm.

≫ Remove the twine from the veal roast. Slice and serve immediately with the carrots and the gin-flavored sauce.

PAN-FRIED VEAL WITH GIROLLE MUSHROOMS

PREPARATION: 30 minutes
COOKING TIME: 1¼ hours

INGREDIENTS

Serves 6

- 1 piece veal flank weighing about 2¾ lb (1.2 kg)
- 1¾ lb (800 g) fresh girolle mushrooms
- 3 shallots
- 3 tbsp vegetable oil
- 2 cups (500 ml) white wine
- 1¼ cups (300 ml) veal broth
- 3½ oz (100 g) hazelnuts
- 3 tbsp walnut oil
- generous 1 tbsp thick crème fraîche
- salt, freshly ground pepper

》Carefully clean the girolle mushrooms. Peel and chop the shallots.

》Cut the meat into medium-size pieces. Heat the vegetable oil in a large saucepan and seal the meat on all sides over high heat. Add the shallots and the girolle mushrooms. Cook for 5 minutes. Pour the white wine over the meat and season with salt and pepper. Bring to a boil, then add the veal broth. Cook, covered, for about 1 hour over medium heat, stirring frequently.

》Meanwhile, coarse crush the hazelnuts then dry-fry them in a skillet for 2 minutes over low heat. Transfer to a plate.

》Heat the walnut oil in the skillet and cook the remaining mushrooms for 3–5 minutes. Season with salt and pepper, and drain in a sieve.

》When the meat is done, take it out of the saucepan. If the sauce is too runny, reduce it before adding the crème fraîche. Bring to a boil and cook for 5 minutes then blend with a hand blender.

》Put the meat and the girolle mushrooms in the sauce, and reheat for a few minutes over low heat. Sprinkle over the fried hazelnuts and serve immediately.

You can replace the girolle mushrooms with wild mushrooms when they are in season (porcini or horn of plenty).

VEAL TARTARE WITH MUSTARD

PREPARATION: **30 minutes**
MARINADE: **30 minutes**
NO COOKING TIME

INGREDIENTS

Serves 6
- 2 lb (900 g) boneless rump roast or center cut of tenderloin
- 4 shallots
- 1 bunch cilantro
- juice of 1 lemon
- 3 tbsp cider vinegar
- 2 tbsp mild mustard
- 2 tbsp soy sauce
- $1/3$ cup (80 ml) olive oil
- 3 tbsp mustard seeds
- salt, freshly ground pepper

⟩ Mince the meat very finely with a knife.

⟩ Peel and chop the shallots. Wash the cilantro and chop the leaves.

⟩ Mix the lemon juice, cider vinegar, salt and pepper, mustard, soy sauce, and the olive oil in a bowl.

⟩ Put the meat in the bowl and add the shallots, cilantro, and the mustard seeds. Stir well, check the seasoning then chill the bowl in the refrigerator for about 30 minutes.

⟩ Divide the veal tartare into 6 portions, and serve with toasted bread slices and a crisp salad.

ROAST VEAL TENDERLOIN WITH PORCINI MUSHROOMS

PREPARATION: **20 minutes**
COOKING TIME: **20 minutes**
STANDING TIME: **15 minutes**

INGREDIENTS

Serves 6

- 2 pieces from center cut of veal tenderloin weighing 1–1¼ lb (500–600 g)
- 14 oz (400 g) porcini mushrooms
- 7 tbsp (100 ml) walnut oil
- 1 bunch flat-leaf parsley
- 20 thin slices smoked lean bacon or belly of pork
- salt, freshly ground pepper

》 Pre-heat the oven to 375 °F (190 °C).

》 Wash and chop the parsley.

》 Clean the mushrooms (rinsing them briefly under running cold water) and coarsely chop. Heat 3½ tbsp (50 ml) walnut oil in a large skillet and cook for 5–7 minutes over high heat. Season with salt and pepper; add the chopped parsley, stir, and allow to cool.

》 Season the veal all over with salt and pepper. Spread the cooked mushrooms over 1 of the tenderloins. Place the second tenderloin on top, positioning it with its tapering side above the wider side of the other. Carefully wrap the slices of bacon around the meat and truss up securely with twine.

》 Put the veal roast in an ovenproof dish and pour the remaining walnut oil over it. Cook in the oven for 20 minutes, basting the roast halfway through.

》 Take the roast out of the oven, wrap tightly in aluminum foil, and allow to rest for 15 minutes.

》 Discard the twine and slice the roast.

TIP

You can serve the roast with a gratin of potatoes or with a mixed vegetable and chestnut purée.

Veal spare ribs with honey and lime

PREPARATION: **15 minutes**
MARINADE: **3 hours**
COOKING TIME: **2 hours**

INGREDIENTS

Serves 6

- 6 bone-in veal spare ribs weighing about 9 oz (250 g) each
- 6 limes
- 1¼ cups (300 ml) veal broth
- 3½ tbsp (100 g) runny lemon blossom honey
- 7 tbsp (100 ml) olive oil
- salt, freshly ground pepper

≫ Rinse 3 limes, grate the rind, and reserve the juice in a glass in the refrigerator.

≫ Mix the rind with the olive oil in a bowl. Season with salt and pepper.

≫ Put the spare ribs in a deep dish. Pour over the marinade and coat the ribs well. Wrap in plastic wrap and marinate for 3 hours in the refrigerator.

≫ Pre-heat the oven to 300 °F (150 °C).

≫ Drain the spare ribs and seal them on all sides without any oil or butter for 4–5 minutes in a hot skillet. Put them in an ovenproof dish.

≫ Skim the fat from the skillet and deglaze it with the lime juice. Add the honey and caramelize slightly. Pour in the veal broth and season with salt and pepper. Bring to a boil, then pour over the spare ribs.

≫ Cover the dish with a sheet of aluminum foil. Cook in the oven for an initial 1 hour 30 minutes, turning the spare ribs every 20 minutes or so.

≫ Meanwhile, wash the other 3 limes and cut in half. Put them, skin-side uppermost, in the ovenproof dish with the partially cooked spare ribs. Increase the temperature to 355 °F (180 °C) and cook for a further 30 minutes, turning the ribs after 15 minutes.

≫ Serve the ribs hot with lemon-flavored couscous or puréed carrots with ginger.

BREAST OF VEAL WITH HERB STUFFING

PREPARATION: **30 minutes**
COOKING TIME: **1 1/2 hours**
STANDING TIME: **15 minutes**

INGREDIENTS

Serves 6

- 1 boneless piece of veal breast, with one side still attached, weighing about 2¾ lb (1.2 kg) (ask your butcher)
- 2 slices sandwich loaf, crusts removed
- 3 tbsp milk
- 1 bunch flat-leaf parsley
- 3 sprigs tarragon
- 1 large onion
- scant 1 lb (400 g) sausage meat
- generous 1 tbsp fennel seeds
- 3 tbsp olive oil
- 2½ tbsp (40 g) butter, chilled
- salt, freshly ground pepper

≫ Pre-heat the oven to 320 °F (160 °C).

≫ Soak the bread in the milk.

≫ Wash and chop the herbs. Peel and chop the onion.

≫ Mix the sausage meat with the chopped onion and herbs, the soaked bread, fennel seeds, and half the olive oil in a bowl. Season with salt and pepper, and stir until the well-blended stuffing holds its shape.

≫ Open the prepared breast of veal as if it were a book, spread the stuffing all over the inside surfaces and truss with twine.

≫ Put the stuffed veal in a flameproof dish and brush with the remaining oil; season with salt and pepper. Cook in the oven for 45 minutes, turning the meat every 10—15 minutes, then increase the oven temperature to 355 °F (180 °C). Pour generous ¾ cup (200 ml) water in the bottom of the dish and cook for a further 45—50 minutes, basting the meat frequently with the cooking juices.

≫ Take the breast of veal out of the oven, wrap in foil, and allow to rest for 15 minutes.

≫ Skim the fat and oil from the dish and heat the remaining cooking liquid over high heat. Add a little water if necessary and reduce to make the gravy. Whisk in the butter and reserve the gravy. Keep warm.

≫ Discard the twine from the meat and slice it. Serve with the gravy. Accompany with glazed young carrots , baked pasta, or baby vegetables.

RIB OF VEAL WITH CIDER SAUCE

PREPARATION: **20 minutes**
COOKING TIME: **50 minutes**
STANDING TIME: **10 minutes**

INGREDIENTS

Serves 6

- 2 thick rib chops weighing generous 1 lb (500–600 g)
- 3 tbsp grapeseed oil + a little for greasing the ovenproof dish
- 14 tbsp (200 g) butter, chilled
- 2 shallots
- 2 cups (500 ml) cider
- 1 cup (250 ml) veal broth
- 2 lb (900 g) garden peas, podded
- salt, freshly ground pepper

≫ Pre-heat the oven to 250 °F (120 °C).

≫ Put the veal in an ovenproof dish that has been lightly greased with grapeseed oil. Brush the meat with grapeseed oil. Dot with 2 tablespoons (30 g) of butter, cut into small pieces; season with salt and pepper. Cook in the oven for 45 minutes, turning halfway through.

≫ Meanwhile, peel and chop the shallots. Melt 1½ tablespoons (20 g) of butter in a large saucepan and cook for 5 minutes. Add the cider and reduce by two-thirds over low heat. Pour in the veal broth and reduce again by half. Whisk in 1½ tablespoons (20 g) of chilled butter, cut into small pieces. Keep the sauce hot in a double boiler, making sure it does not boil.

≫ Cook the garden peas in a large saucepan full of boiling salted water for 15 minutes. Drain (reserving a little of their cooking liquid) then blend with a hand blender until smooth with the remaining butter, cut into pieces, and salt and pepper (add a little of the cooking liquid if the mixture is too thick). Keep hot in a double boiler.

≫ When the meat is done, switch the oven to broiler mode and brown the veal for 5 minutes.

≫ Take the meat out of the oven, wrap in aluminum foil, and allow to rest for 10 minutes.

≫ Slice the meat and serve with the cider sauce and the garden pea purée.

VEAL SHANK WITH PICKLED LEMONS

PREPARATION: **15 minutes**
COOKING TIME: **1 hour**
40 minutes

INGREDIENTS

Serves 6
- 6 thick slices from center cut of veal shank (osso buco pieces)
- 2 large red onions
- 3 tbsp olive oil
- 3½ tbsp (100 g) lemon blossom honey
- 2 cups (500 ml) veal broth
- 4 very small salt-pickled lemons
- salt, freshly ground pepper

≫ Peel and thinly slice the onions.

≫ Heat the olive oil in a flameproof dish over medium heat and seal and brown the veal slices, allowing 5 minutes for each side.

≫ Add the onions and pour in the honey. Caramelize slightly before pouring in the veal broth. Season with salt and pepper.

≫ Cover the veal slices with a large sheet of siliconized paper and simmer over low heat for 45 minutes.

≫ Rinse the pickled lemons under cold running water, slice if necessary, then add to the saucepan. Turn the veal slices and cook for a further 45 minutes over low heat, when the meat should be very tender and easily detached from the bone (do not hesitate to add a little hot water if necessary, to keep the veal slices covered). Serve very hot, on the bone.

You can serve this veal dish with a couscous of semolina and raisins, flavored with orange juice and cilantro.

Mushrooms and Camembert cheese in veal parcels

PREPARATION: **40 minutes**
COOKING TIME: **30 minutes**

INGREDIENTS

Serves 6

- 6 large veal escalopes
- 9 oz (250 g) button mushrooms
- 2 sprigs flat-leaf parsley
- 2½ tbsp (40 g) butter
- 1 lb (400 g) sausage meat
- 4 oz (120 g) underripe Camembert cheese, peeled and diced
- 3 shallots
- 3 tbsp vegetable oil
- 1 ²/₃ cups (400 ml) cider
- 1 cup (250 ml) veal broth
- 2 tbsp thick crème fraîche
- salt, freshly ground pepper

》 Clean and coarsely chop the mushrooms. Rinse and chop the parsley.

》 Melt the butter in a skillet and cook the mushrooms for 10 minutes over medium heat. Season with salt and pepper, and add the parsley. Mix well.

》 In a large bowl, mix the mushrooms with the sausage meat and the diced Camembert cheese.

》 Divide this stuffing into six equal portions. Place a portion of stuffing in the center of each escalope and wrap up in the veal to form a parcel; tie up carefully with twine.

》 Peel and chop the shallots. Heat the oil in a flameproof dish and seal and lightly brown the veal parcels all over, turning them every 2 minutes. Add the shallots and cook for 3 minutes. Pour in the cider, bring to a boil, and cook for 5 minutes. Add the veal broth and season with salt and pepper. Cover and simmer gently for 20 minutes over low heat.

》 Take the veal parcels out of the dish and boil the cooking liquid until it has reduced by two-thirds. Add the crème fraîche and reduce further to obtain a smooth, velvety sauce. Blend with a hand blender.

》 Reheat the veal parcels for 3 minutes in the sauce and serve with an accompaniment of rice or ribbon noodles.

CORDON-BLEU VEAL WITH PARMESAN CHEESE

PREPARATION: 30 minutes
COOKING TIME: 20 minutes

INGREDIENTS

Serves 6

- 6 large veal escalopes (cut from leg center roast)
- 4 oz (120 g) Parmesan cheese, in one piece
- 12 basil leaves
- 6 slices Parma ham
- 3 eggs
- ²/₃ cup (100 g) all-purpose flour
- 1½ cups (180 g) fine breadcrumbs
- 7 tbsp (100 ml) olive oil
- 3½ tbsp (50 g) butter
- salt, freshly ground pepper

≫ Pre-heat the oven to 350 °F (180 °C).

≫ Cut the piece of Parmesan cheese into shavings, using a knife or a vegetable peeler. Wash the basil leaves and snip them into small pieces with scissors.

≫ Place the escalopes between 2 layers of plastic wrap and pound them with the base of a saucepan to flatten them.

≫ Remove the plastic wrap and spread the escalopes out flat on the work surface. Season with salt and pepper. Place 1 slice of Parma ham on each escalope and scatter the Parmesan shavings and the basil leaves on top. Fold the escalopes in half, pressing down gently to make them adhere.

≫ Beat the eggs lightly in a fairly deep dish. Spread out the flour on another plate and the breadcrumbs on a third plate. Cover each escalope with flour then dip in the beaten egg and finally coat with the breadcrumbs.

≫ Using a very large skillet (or 2 medium-size skillets) heat the olive oil and the butter over moderate heat and fry the escalopes for 5–7 minutes on each side, to cook and brown.

≫ Place the cordon-bleu escalopes in a single layer in a large ovenproof dish, pre-heated and lined with siliconized paper. Place in the pre-heated oven to finish cooking for 6–8 minutes. Serve immediately, with a tomato salad dressed with balsamic vinegar and garlic.

SLOW-FRIED TENDER BREAST OF VEAL WITH CILANTRO AND TOMATO SALSA

PREPARATION: **30 minutes**
COOKING TIME: **40 minutes**

INGREDIENTS

Serves 6

- 6 slices from boneless middle cut of veal breast weighing about 7 oz (200 g) each
- 3 medium tomatoes
- 4 large shallots
- 3 sprigs cilantro
- $^2/_3$–¾ cup (150–200 ml) olive oil
- 12 baby carrots
- 1 bunch scallions
- 6 baby leeks
- salt, freshly ground black pepper

≫ Make the salsa: wash and quarter the tomatoes, de-seed, and cut the flesh into small cubes. Peel and chop the shallots. Use scissors to snip the cilantro leaves into small pieces. Mix the tomato cubes with the shallots and cilantro in a bowl; season with salt and pepper, and stir in 7 tablespoons (100 ml) of olive oil. Chill in the refrigerator.

≫ Peel the carrots, the scallions, and the leeks. Heat a cast-iron broiler griddle over low heat and grill the leeks, turning them frequently. Add the carrots, followed by the scallions, and grill for about 30 minutes, basting with oil at regular intervals and turning frequently.

≫ Meanwhile, season the slices of veal breast all over with salt and pepper; pour just enough olive oil into a large flameproof dish to cover the bottom of the dish and add the slices of veal. Cook for a total of 30–40 minutes over medium heat at first then reduce the heat to low; keep turning the pieces of veal every 6–8 minutes.

≫ Arrange the veal slices and broiled vegetables on individual plates. Spoon the salsa over each portion and serve immediately.

Ensure that the meat is meltingly tender by placing a lid on the dish during the first half of the cooking time.

Veal escalopes Milan-style

PREPARATION: **30 minutes**
COOKING TIME: **20 minutes**

INGREDIENTS

Serves 6

- 6 fairly thick escalopes, sliced
  from leg center roast cut,
  weighing about 7 oz (200 g) each
- 2 cups (500 ml) veal broth
- 3 sprigs lemon thyme
- 3½ tbsp (50 g) butter, chilled
- 2 eggs
- 9 tbsp (80 g) all-purpose flour
- 1¾ cups (200 g) fine breadcrumbs
- 1¼ lb (600 g) spaghetti
- 1 quart (1 liter) oil for deep frying
- salt, freshly ground pepper

≫ Reduce the volume of the veal broth by one-third, boiling it in a saucepan with the sprigs of thyme and a seasoning of salt and pepper. Reduce the heat to medium and gradually whisk in pieces of the cold butter. Keep this sauce hot making sure it does not boil.

≫ Lightly beat the eggs in a bowl. Spread out the flour and breadcrumbs separately on two plates. Season the escalopes with salt and pepper before coating them with flour, then with beaten egg, and finally with breadcrumbs.

≫ Cook the spaghetti in a large saucepan of boiling salted water for 10–12 minutes.

≫ Heat the oil for deep-frying in a large saucepan or deep-fryer. When the oil is very hot (350 °F (180 °C) maximum), lower the escalopes into it two at a time and fry for 5 minutes. Drain on absorbent paper towels.

≫ Drain the spaghetti and place in a hot serving dish. Pour the hot veal and thyme sauce all over them. Serve at once with the veal escalopes.

You can also use flavored breadcrumbs: try mixing with finely grated lemon rind or 1 tablespoon of chopped thyme.

BRAISED RUMP OF VEAL WITH ROSEMARY

PREPARATION: **30 minutes**
COOKING TIME: **1¼ hours**
STANDING TIME: **15 minutes**

INGREDIENTS

Serves 6

- 2¾ lb (1.2 kg) rump of veal, cut into large cubes if preferred
- 2 large bunches scallions
- 3 carrots
- 3 tbsp olive oil
- 1 ⅔ cups (400 ml) dry white wine
- 1¼ cups (300 ml) veal broth
- 2 large sprigs rosemary
- salt, freshly ground pepper

≫ Pre-heat the oven to 350 °F (180 °C).

≫ Peel the scallions, leaving the bulbs whole and some of the green stalk attached.

≫ Peel the carrots and slice into rounds or dice.

≫ Heat the oil in a flameproof dish and brown the veal until well colored over high heat. Season with salt and pepper. Add the scallions and the carrots, positioning these near the outside edge of the dish, and cook them for 2 minutes. Pour in the wine, bring to a boil, and cook for 5 minutes.

≫ Pour in the veal broth, bring to a boil, and add the sprigs of rosemary; season with salt and pepper. Cover and place in the oven. Cook, undisturbed, in the oven for 1 hour 15 minutes.

≫ Take the dish out of the oven and allow to rest for 15 minutes before serving.

TIP

You can serve this braised veal dish with a homemade ratatouille flavored with fresh herbs.

VEAL STEW WITH BABY ONIONS, TARRAGON, AND CREAM

PREPARATION: **45 minutes**
COOKING TIME: **1¹/₂ hours**

INGREDIENTS

Serves 6
- 3¼ lb (1.5 kg) boneless shoulder of veal, cut into large pieces
- 1 large onion
- 2 cloves
- 2 carrots
- 2 sticks celery
- 1 leek
- 1 bouquet garni
- few peppercorns
- 1 large bunch scallions
- 4 tbsp (60 g) butter
- 1 tbsp granulated sugar
- 2 cups (500 ml) light cream
- scant 1 tsp cornstarch
- 1 bunch tarragon
- salt, freshly ground pepper

》 Peel the onion and stud it with the cloves. Peel, trim and wash the carrots, celery, and leek.

》 Place the veal in a large flameproof dish, cover with cold water, bring to a boil and boil for 1 minute. Drain the meat and rinse under cold running water. Clean the dish and return the meat to it. Add the prepared vegetables, bouquet garni, a few peppercorns, and a little salt. Pour in enough cold water to cover all the contents and bring to a boil. Skim any scum, cover, and cook for 1 hour 15 minutes over medium heat. (Continue skimming the surface at regular intervals.)

》 Meanwhile, peel the scallions. Place them in a saucepan with 1½ tablespoons (20 g) of butter, the sugar, and a little salt and pepper. Pour in just enough water to cover. Cover with a sheet of siliconized paper and cook for 15 minutes over medium heat. Cool the scallions in their cooking water.

》 When the meat is done, allow it to rest for 15 minutes in its cooking liquid.

》 Strain 1 quart (1 liter) of the cooking liquid into a flameproof dish and boil for 10 minutes over high heat. Reduce the heat to medium, pour in the cream, and reduce for 15–20 minutes. Mix the cornstarch with a little cold water and stir into the broth and cream mixture, followed by the remaining butter. Stir well, then process with a hand blender.

》 Chop the tarragon leaves. Drain the veal pieces and place in the sauce. Add the tarragon leaves and the drained onions (discard their cooking liquid).

》 Keep the veal hot in the dish in a bain-marie in the oven or over extremely low heat on the stove; do not allow to boil. Serve with a rice pilaf or fresh pasta.

LAMB CUTLETS WITH PARMESAN CHEESE CRUST AND OLIVE GRAVY

PREPARATION: **30 minutes**
COOKING TIME: **25 minutes**
STANDING TIME: **10 minutes**

INGREDIENTS

Serves 6

- 3 racks of lamb or loin of lamb with 6 cutlets each, prepared by your butcher
- 3 tbsp olive oil
- 10 basil leaves
- 4 oz (120 g) finely grated Parmesan cheese
- 3 oz (90 g) breadcrumbs
- 1 egg white
- 1 tbsp mild mustard
- 1 $^2/_3$ cups (400 ml) lamb broth
- 1½ tbsp (25 g) butter, chilled
- 4 oz (120 g) small black olives, pitted
- salt, freshly ground pepper

》 Pre-heat the oven to 355 °F (180 °C).

》 Heat the olive oil in a skillet and seal the sides and underside of the racks of lamb over high heat for 1 minute, and the fatty side of the racks also for 1 minute. Season with salt and pepper. Place on a rack, dab off excess oil with absorbent paper towels, and leave to cool.

》 Snip the basil leaves with scissors.

》 Mix the Parmesan cheese, breadcrumbs, egg white, mustard, and basil in a bowl. Smear this mixture over the fatty side of the racks, pressing down well so it adheres properly.

》 Put the meat in an ovenproof dish, with the crust uppermost. Cook in the oven for 15—20 minutes, depending on whether you like your meat rare, medium, or well done.

》 Meanwhile, pour the lamb broth in a large saucepan and reduce by two-thirds, seasoning with salt and pepper, over low heat.

》 Take the lamb out of the oven, cover with aluminum foil, and rest it for 10 minutes.

》 Away from the heat, when the lamb broth has reduced, whisk in the butter, cut into small pieces, and add the olives.

》 Slice between the cutlets, carving carefully so that the crust remains attached. Serve with the olive-flavored gravy.

LAMB SHOULDER STUFFED WITH DRY FRUITS

PREPARATION: **30 minutes**
COOKING TIME: **55 minutes**
STANDING TIME: **15 minutes**

INGREDIENTS

Serves 6

- 1 lamb shoulder, boneless, weighing about 2¾ lb (1.2 kg)
- 5 large dry figs
- 8 large dry apricots
- 1 large yellow onion
- 2 cloves garlic
- 7 tbsp (100 ml) olive oil
- 1 tsp five-spice powder
- 2 pinches cinnamon
- 2 pinches cumin
- 1 oz (25 g) green walnuts
- 1 oz (25 g) whole almonds
- 1 oz (25 g) hazelnuts
- salt, freshly ground pepper

》 Pre-heat the oven to 355 °F (180 °C).

》 Cut the figs and apricots into very small pieces.

》 Peel and chop the onion and the garlic cloves. Heat 3½ tablespoons (50 ml) of olive oil in a skillet and cook them for 10 minutes over low heat. Season with salt and pepper. Add all the spices, the figs, and apricots. Mix well and allow to cool.

》 Coarsely chop the green walnuts, almonds, and hazelnuts. Add them to the mixture.

》 Open out the lamb shoulder in two. Season the inside with salt and pepper. Stuff with the dry fruit mixture and truss up tightly with twine.

》 Put the lamb in an ovenproof dish and pour over the remaining olive oil. Cook in the oven for 45–50 minutes, turning the shoulder every 15 minutes, and basting it with the cooking juices.

》 Take the lamb shoulder out of the oven, wrap in aluminum foil, and allow to rest for 15 minutes.

》 Thinly slice the meat and serve immediately.

THAI GREEN CURRY WITH LAMB

PREPARATION: 30 minutes
COOKING TIME: 1½ hours

INGREDIENTS

Serves 6
- 3¼ lb (1.5 kg) lamb shoulder,
  cut into bite-size pieces
- 2 yellow onions
- 3 cloves garlic
- 3 tbsp olive oil
- 3 tbsp Thai green curry paste
  (available from Asian grocers)
- 1 ⅔ cups (400 ml) coconut milk
- 4 sprigs cilantro
- salt

❯ Peel and chop the onions and garlic cloves.

❯ Heat the olive oil in a very large saucepan and seal the lamb pieces on all sides over high heat. Transfer to a plate.

❯ Put the onions and garlic in the saucepan and cook for 5 minutes over low heat. Add the Thai green curry paste and some salt. Cook, stirring continuously, for 3 minutes over high heat.

❯ Put the meat back in the saucepan and stir well to coat. Pour in the coconut milk and add enough water to cover the meat. Bring to a boil. Cook, covered, for 1 hour 30 minutes over low heat.

❯ Take the meat out of the saucepan and blend the sauce with a hand blender. Check the seasoning.

❯ Gently reheat the meat in the sauce (making sure it does not boil), adding the cilantro, snipped with scissors. Serve immediately.

This green curry can be served with Thai rice: Cook the rice in water first, heat a little olive oil in a skillet, then gently fry the rice in it with 1 pinch each turmeric and green cardamom and a few slivered almonds.

LAMB TENDERLOIN FILLET WITH MUSTARD

PREPARATION: **30 minutes**
COOKING TIME: **40 minutes**
STANDING TIME: **10 minutes**

INGREDIENTS

Serves 6

- 3 lamb tenderloins
- 3¼ lb (1.5 kg) chard
- 1 ²/₃ cups (400 ml) lamb broth
- 1 bunch savory
- 3 tbsp mustard
- 5½ oz (150 g) breadcrumbs
- ½ egg white
- 3 tbsp olive oil
- salt, freshly ground pepper

> Set aside the chard leaves (and use in another recipe). Peel the stems and cut them into short, fairly wide pieces. Put them in a large saucepan filled with boiling salted water and cook for 25 minutes.

> Meanwhile, pour the lamb broth into a large saucepan. Add two-thirds of the savory leaves, season with salt and pepper, and reduce by half.

> Pre-heat the oven to 355 °F (180 °C). Chop the remaining savory. Mix the mustard, breadcrumbs, egg white, and chopped savory in a bowl. Season with salt and pepper.

> Heat the olive oil in a skillet and seal all the surfaces of the lamb tenderloins over high heat for 1 minute. Pat dry with absorbent paper towels.

> Use an equal amount of the savory-flavored breadcrumb mixture to coat each lamb tenderloin completely and press to make it adhere. Place carefully in a roasting pan lined with siliconized paper. Cook in the oven for 10–15 minutes, depending on whether you like your meat rare, medium, or well done.

> Drain the chard and place in a skillet. Pour in the reduced lamb gravy and reheat over low heat.

> Take the lamb tenderloin fillets out of the oven, cover with aluminum foil, and allow to rest for 10 minutes.

> Slice the meat carefully, so that the crust remains attached

BRAISED LAMB SHANKS WITH SAFFRON

PREPARATION: 20 minutes
COOKING TIME: 1 hour
50 minutes

INGREDIENTS

Serves 6

- 6 lamb shanks
- 2 yellow onions
- 2 cloves garlic
- 3 tbsp olive oil
- 4 oz (120 g) runny honey
- generous 3 pinches saffron
- 1²/₃ cups (400 ml) lamb broth (or water)
- 7 oz (200 g) large raisins
- 3 tbsp rose water
- salt, freshly ground pepper

≫ Peel and thinly slice the onion and garlic cloves.

≫ Heat the olive oil in a very large saucepan and seal the lamb shanks on all sides over high heat. Transfer to a plate. Put the onions and garlic in the saucepan and cook for 5 minutes over medium heat.

≫ Put the lamb shanks back in the saucepan. Pour over the honey, season with salt and pepper, and caramelize slightly, stirring the meat to ensure it is well coated. Add the saffron and the lamb broth (or water). Cook, covered, for 1 hour over low heat, turning the lamb shanks every 15 minutes.

≫ Meanwhile, soak the raisins in a bowl containing 7 table-spoons (100 ml) of lukewarm water mixed with the rose water.

≫ Add the raisins and rose water to the saucepan after 1 hour's cooking time and cook for a further 40–50 minutes: the meat should come off the bone easily.

≫ Take the meat out of the saucepan and reduce the sauce slightly over high heat.

≫ Put the lamb shanks back in the sauce and simmer for a few minutes. Serve with fine semolina couscous and broiled vegetables.

LAMB-STUFFED EGGPLANTS

PREPARATION: 40 minutes
COOKING TIME: 1½ hours

INGREDIENTS

Serves 6
- 2¼ lb (1 kg) leftover slow-cooked lamb (shoulder, leg) or lamb shoulder cooked in a tagine
- 3 large round or long eggplants
- 7 oz (200 g) pine nuts
- 2 tomatoes
- 2 yellow onions
- 4 oz (120 g) grated Parmesan cheese
- 2 tbsp cumin seeds
- ⅔ cup (150 ml) olive oil
- salt, freshly ground pepper

≫ Pre-heat the oven to 355 °F (180 °C).

≫ Wash the eggplants and cut them in half lengthways. Put them in an ovenproof dish. Score the flesh into a crisscross pattern with the blade of a knife. Pour over 7 tablespoons (100 ml) of olive oil and season with salt and pepper. Cover the dish with aluminum foil and cook in the oven for 35–40 minutes.

≫ Tear the cooked meat into shreds.

≫ Scald the tomatoes for 20 seconds in boiling water then plunge into a bowl of cold water. Drain, remove the skins, de-seed and crush.

≫ Peel and thinly slice the onions. Heat the remaining olive oil in a skillet and cook them for 10 minutes over low heat. Add the pine nuts and brown for 3 minutes.

≫ Add the crushed tomatoes to the skillet, followed by the meat, cumin seeds, and 1 large glass water. Stir then cook for 15 minutes over low heat.

≫ Take the eggplants out of the oven (keeping it switched on) and allow to cool. Carefully scoop out the flesh with a spoon and chop it with a knife. Stir it into the tomato and meat mixture.

≫ Stuff the eggplants with the mixture then sprinkle grated Parmesan cheese over the top. Place in the ovenproof dish once more.

≫ Put the stuffed eggplants in the oven to reheat and brown for 25–30 minutes. Serve very hot.

Garlic lamb noisettes

PREPARATION: **30 minutes**
SOAKING TIME: **overnight**
COOKING TIME: **2¼ hours**

INGREDIENTS

Serves 6

- 2¼ lb (1 kg) lamb tenderloin,
  from rib chop cut, fat removed
- 1¼ lb (600 g) dry garbanzo beans
- 1 onion, peeled
- 1 carrot, peeled
- 1 bay leaf
- 2 heads garlic
- 7 tbsp (100 ml) olive oil
- 1 ²/₃ cups (400 ml) lamb broth
- 10 tbsp butter (140 g) butter
- 1 level tbsp cumin
- salt, freshly ground pepper

》 The day before, soak the garbanzo beans in a large bowl of cold water.

》 The next day, drain and rinse the garbanzo beans, then place in a large saucepan. Add the onion, carrot, and bay leaf. Pour in 2 quarts + 2 cups (2.5 liters) cold water to cover. Bring to a boil then cook for 1 hour 30 minutes over low heat.

》 Pre-heat the oven to 320 °F (160 °C). Separate the garlic cloves and keep them whole and unpeeled. Spread them out in a large ovenproof dish. Pour over 3 tablespoons of olive oil and season with salt and pepper. Cook in the oven for 30 minutes.

》 Meanwhile, pour the lamb broth into a large saucepan. Season with salt and pepper and reduce by half over medium heat. Whisk in 1½ tablespoons (25 g) of butter, cut into dice. Keep this gravy hot, but make sure it does not boil.

》 Drain the garbanzo beans, then place in a food processor bowl with the remaining butter and the cumin. Season with salt and pepper. Process at low speed for 3 minutes until you have a smooth mixture. Keep hot in a double boiler.

》 Take the garlic cloves out of the oven (keeping it switched on) and arrange them around the inside edge of the ovenproof dish. Carve the meat into slices ¾ inch (2 cm) thick. Season with salt and pepper. Heat the remaining oil in a skillet and seal the lamb noisettes over high heat. Put these in the center of the dish containing the garlic cloves. Cook in the oven for 6—8 minutes (for meat that is pink in the center).

》 Serve the garlic lamb noisettes with the garbanzo bean purée and the gravy.

LAMB CUTLET CREPINETTES

PREPARATION: **30 minutes**
COOKING TIME: **45 minutes**

INGREDIENTS

Serves 6

- 12 prime lamb cutlets, prepared by your butcher
- 1 large onion
- 1 small red chile
- 4 sprigs cilantro
- 7 tbsp (100 ml) olive oil
- ½ tsp coriander
- 2 pinches cumin
- 2 pinches ginger
- 7 oz (200 g) lamb's or pig's caul fat
- salt

≫ Peel and thinly slice the onion. Cut the chile in half, de-seed, and thinly chop. Snip the cilantro with scissors.

≫ Heat 3½ tbsp (50 ml) olive oil in a skillet and fry the onion and the chile over medium heat, stirring frequently. Add the spices, season with salt, and pour in ²/₃ cup (150 ml) water. Cook for a further 15–20 minutes. Add the snipped cilantro and allow to cool. Blend everything in a small food processor until you obtain a coarse paste.

≫ Season the lamb cutlets with salt. Spread the chile paste on one side of them.

≫ Rinse the caul and cut it into 12 pieces. Carefully wrap each cutlet in a piece of caul fat.

≫ Heat the remaining oil in a large skillet and cook the cutlets for 5–8 minutes on each side.

> You can serve the lamb cutlet crepinettes with *pipérade* (a Basque egg dish made with onion, green bell peppers, tomatoes, and chiles) or an eggplant mousse.

LAMB TAGINE WITH ORANGES AND ALMONDS

PREPARATION: **30 minutes**
COOKING TIME: **1³/₄ hours**

INGREDIENTS

Serves 6
- 3½ lb (1.6 kg) lamb shoulder, cut into pieces
- 2 yellow onions
- 3 tbsp olive oil
- generous 3 tbsp orange marmalade
- 1 pinch saffron strands
- juice of 3 oranges
- 3 tbsp orange flower water
- 5 oz (150 g) whole almonds
- 1 unwaxed orange
- 1¾ oz (50 g) runny honey
- salt, freshly ground pepper

》 Peel and thinly slice the onions.

》 Heat the olive oil in a large saucepan or tagine, and seal the meat pieces on all sides. Transfer to a plate. Put the onions in the saucepan and cook for 10 minutes over low heat.

》 Put the meat back in the saucepan or tagine. Add the marmalade and saffron, then season with salt and pepper. Cook for 5 minutes over medium heat, ensuring the meat pieces are well coated in the marmalade. Pour in the orange juice and orange flower water. Add sufficient cold water to cover the meat. Cook, covered, for 1 hour 30 minutes over low heat, stirring frequently.

》 Dry-fry the almonds in a skillet.

》 Rinse the orange (but do not peel it) and cut it into 12 segments. Heat the honey in a skillet until it caramelizes slightly, and cook the orange segments in the honey for a few minutes over low heat.

》 After the meat has been cooking for 1 hour 30 minutes, add the almonds and orange segments to the saucepan or tagine and cook, uncovered, for 15 minutes over low heat. The meat should be very tender.

Lamb and garden pea stew

PREPARATION: **40 minutes**
COOKING TIME: **1¾ hours**

INGREDIENTS

Serves 6

- 2¾ lb (1.2 kg) lamb shoulder, cut
  into bite-size pieces
- 2 lb (900 g) neck slices of lamb,
  boneless
- 1 onion
- 3 tbsp olive oil
- ½ cup (70 g) all-purpose flour
- 1 tbsp tomato paste
- 2 cups (500 ml) white wine
- 14 oz (400 g) canned peeled
  tomatoes
- 2 sprigs thyme
- 1 bay leaf
- generous 1 lb (500 g) small
  turnips
- 2 tbsp (30 g) butter
- 1¾ lb (800 g) garden peas,
  podded (fresh or frozen)
- salt, freshly ground pepper

≫ Peel and thinly slice the onion. Heat the olive oil in a large
saucepan and seal all the pieces of meat over high heat.
Season with salt and pepper. Add the onion and brown for
3 minutes over medium heat. Sprinkle with the flour and mix
well to ensure that the meat pieces and onions are coated.
Add the tomato paste and cook for 2 minutes over high heat.

≫ Pour in the white wine and add the canned tomatoes. Bring
to a boil then add enough cold water to cover the meat.
Add the thyme and bay leaf. Simmer, covered, for 1 hour
30 minutes over medium heat.

≫ Meanwhile, peel the turnips and cut into pieces. Put them
in a flameproof dish with the butter and season with salt
and pepper. Cover with water. Cook, covered with a sheet of
siliconized paper, for 15 minutes over medium heat.

≫ Plunge the garden peas into a saucepan filled with boiling
salted water. Drain then refresh under running cold water.

≫ After the stew has been cooking for 1 hour 30 minutes, add
the turnips and cook for a final 15 minutes, stirring in the peas
3 minutes before this time is up. Serve immediately.

SLOW-COOKED LEG OF LAMB WITH THYME

PREPARATION: **30 minutes**
COOKING TIME: **7 hours**

INGREDIENTS

Serves 6

- 1 boned leg of lamb weighing 3½ lb (1.6 kg)
- 2 carrots
- 1 stick celery
- 2 tomatoes
- 2 onions
- 1 tbsp olive oil
- 1 head garlic
- 1 bouquet garni
- 1 ⅔ cups (400 ml) chicken broth
- 1 ⅔ cups (400 ml) white wine
- 1 large bunch thyme
- salt, freshly ground pepper

≫ Pre-heat the oven to 250 °F (120 °C).

≫ Peel the carrots and cut into small dice. Peel, trim, and thinly slice the celery stick. Wash the tomatoes and cut into quarters.

≫ Peel and thinly slice the onions. Separate the garlic cloves and keep them whole and unpeeled.

≫ Heat the oil in a deep flameproof dish and brown the leg of lamb all over for 2–3 minutes over high heat. Add the carrots, celery stick, bouquet garni, garlic cloves, tomatoes, and onions. Season with salt and pepper, then pour in the chicken broth and the white wine. Place sprigs of thyme under, around, and on top of the leg of lamb.

≫ Cook, covered, in the oven for about 7 hours, basting the meat frequently: the leg of lamb is ready to eat when it is tender enough to be cut with a spoon.

≫ Serve the leg of lamb with crushed potatoes and garlic-fried green beans.

For an unusual, unexpected flavor, add a handful of clean, fresh hay with the thyme: it goes very well with the leg of lamb.

TAPENADE-STUFFED SADDLE OF LAMB

PREPARATION: **30 minutes**
COOKING TIME: **1 hour**
STANDING TIME: **15 minutes**

INGREDIENTS

Serves 6

- 2¾ lb (1.2 kg) saddle of lamb, boneless (the top of the hind-quarters: the traditional French butcher's saddle of lamb)
- 10 basil leaves
- 3 tbsp black olive tapenade
- 2¼ lb (1 kg) fava beans, podded (fresh or frozen)
- 1 bunch thyme
- 2½ cups (600 ml) lamb broth
- 2 tbsp (30 g) butter, chilled
- 3 tbsp olive oil
- salt, freshly ground pepper

› Pre-heat the oven to 355 °F (180 °C).

› Chop the basil leaves. Mix them with the tapenade in a bowl. Cut open the saddle of lamb lengthways like a book. Spread the inside with the basil-flavored tapenade; close and truss up with twine.

› Put the stuffed saddle of lamb in an ovenproof dish. Season with salt and pepper, and pour over the olive oil. Cook in the oven for 40–45 minutes, turning the meat over and basting it every 10 minutes.

› Meanwhile, pour the lamb broth into a saucepan and season with salt and pepper. Reduce by two-thirds over medium heat.

› Cook the fava beans for 8 minutes in a large saucepan filled with boiling salted water. Drain and refresh in a bowl of cold water. If you are using fresh fava beans, skin them carefully without crushing.

› Take the saddle of lamb out of the oven, wrap in aluminum foil, and allow to rest for 15 minutes.

› When the lamb broth has reduced, add the butter, cut into pieces. Blend the sauce in a food processor or with a hand blender, then add the thyme leaves. Pour the thyme-flavored sauce into a large skillet and heat gently. Add the fava beans and simmer for 10 minutes without boiling.

› Carefully carve the saddle of lamb into slices and serve immediately with the fava beans in thyme-flavored gravy.

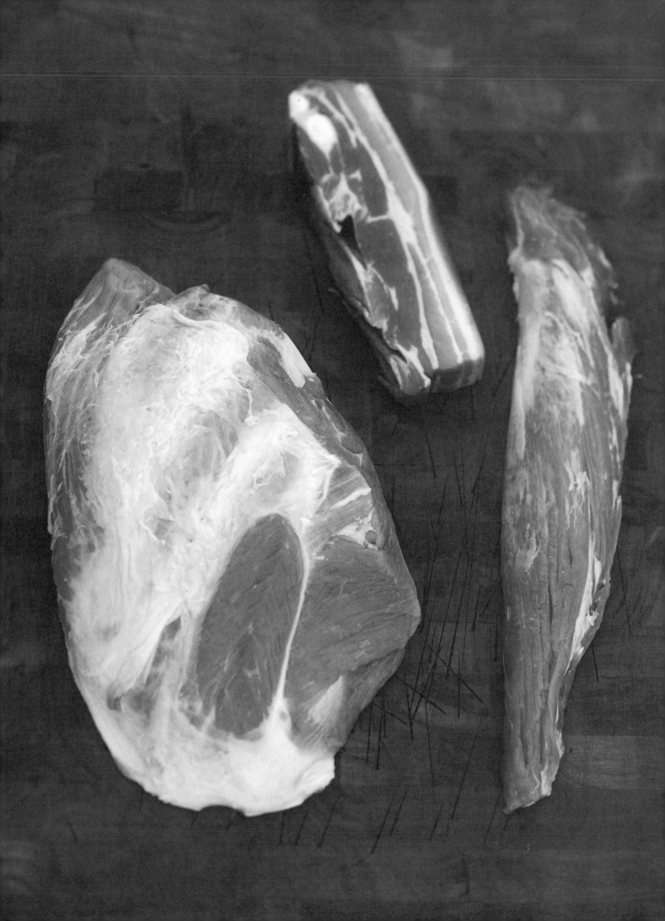

HONEY-ROAST PORK COOKED IN CANNING JARS

PREPARATION: **20 minutes**
COOKING TIME: **3 hours**
STANDING TIME: **2 days**

INGREDIENTS

Serves 6
- 2¾ lb (1.2 kg) pork, boneless loin roast with some fat left on it
- 7 tbsp (100 ml) olive oil
- 4 tbsp runny honey
- 2 tbsp cilantro seeds
- 2 tbsp cumin seeds
- salt, freshly ground pepper

》 Wash 2 canning jars with their lids, screw collars, and rubber sealing rings before lowering them into a canning (preserving) pan of boiling water to sterilize them. Drain them upside down—but do not dry with a kitchen cloth—and leave to cool.

》 Pour half the olive oil and honey into the bottom of each jar, adding half the cilantro and cumin seeds and a pinch of salt and pepper.

》 Slice the pork in half. Place half in each jar, leaving a space of about ¾ inch (2 cm) between the top of the meat and the lid's screw threads on the jar. Pour the remaining oil and honey over the top of the meat, followed by the cilantro and cumin seeds. Season with a pinch each of salt and pepper. Make sure the rubber seals are correctly positioned when sealing the jars.

》 Place the jars in a canning (preserving) pan, add more than enough water to cover them, and heat to 210–230 °F (100–110 °C). Cook for 3 hours, keeping the temperature of the water at a constant 210–230 °F (100–110 °C).

》 Carefully remove the jars from the water and allow to cool completely. Store in the refrigerator and wait for at least 2 days before consuming (unopened, the meat will keep for several weeks).

》 Serve the pork cold, with best-quality mustard, pickled onions, gherkins, and rustic artisan bread.

Pork tenderloin with Sichuan pepper coating

PREPARATION: **40 minutes**
COOKING TIME: **30 minutes**
STANDING TIME: **5 minutes**

INGREDIENTS

Serves 6

- 2 pieces pork tenderloin weighing
  1–1¼ lb (500–600 g) each
- 24 small green or purple
  asparagus spears
- 1¼ lb (600 g) shiitake
  mushrooms, cleaned
- ²/₃ cup (150 ml) maple syrup
- ¹/₃ cup (80 g) butter
- 3 tbsp olive oil
- 3 tbsp coarse crushed Sichuan
  peppercorns
- salt, freshly ground pepper

≫ Pre-heat the oven to 320 °F (160 °C).

≫ Trim and wash the asparagus and then cook them for 5 minutes in a saucepan filled with boiling salted water. Drain and refresh under cold running water.

≫ Spread out the crushed Sichuan pepper on a large plate. Cut each of the tenderloins into 3 steaks. Heat the olive oil in a skillet and seal the steaks all over for 2 minutes. Sprinkle them with the maple syrup and cook for 6–8 minutes over medium heat, spooning the syrupy liquid over repeatedly to glaze them.

≫ Take the pork steaks out of the skillet, reserving the cooking liquid in the skillet, and roll them in the pepper, pressing lightly. Place them on a baking tray lined with siliconized paper. Cook in the oven for 6–8 minutes.

≫ Meanwhile, add 2½ tablespoons (40 g) of butter to the liquid in the skillet and cook the shiitake mushrooms for 5–7 minutes over medium heat. Sprinkle with a pinch of salt.

≫ Melt the remaining butter in another skillet and fry the asparagus for 3 minutes over medium heat. Season with salt and pepper.

≫ Take the pork steaks out of the oven, cover with a piece of aluminum foil, and rest them for 5 minutes. Serve with the asparagus and the mushrooms.

ROAST BELLY OF PORK WITH FRESH FIGS

PREPARATION: 20 minutes
MARINADE: 4 hours
COOKING TIME: 2½ hours
STANDING TIME: 15 minutes

INGREDIENTS

Serves 6

- 3¼ lb (1.5 kg) belly of pork in one piece
- 12 ripe fresh figs
- 2¼ lb (1 kg) celeriac
- generous 1 tbsp five-spice powder
- 3 tbsp sweet soy sauce
- 3 tbsp soy sauce
- 3 tbsp rice wine vinegar (or wine vinegar)
- 3½ tbsp (100 g) runny honey
- ²/₃ cup (150 g) butter
- salt, freshly ground pepper

》Remove the skin from the belly of pork. Score the underlying fat with a cross-hatched pattern using a knife.

》Warm the honey with the two types of soy sauce, the vinegar, and five-spice powder. Season with a small pinch each of salt and pepper.

》Place the belly of pork in a deep dish, fat side uppermost. Sprinkle with the marinade and brush to coat all the surfaces of the meat with it. Cover with plastic wrap and chill in the refrigerator for 4 hours, turning the belly of pork after 2 hours.

》Pre-heat the broiler in the oven to 350 °F (180 °C).

》Place the marinated pork, fat side uppermost, on a rack over a drip tray into which you have poured 1 cup (250 ml) of water. Position near the bottom of the oven. Broil the pork for 1 hour 30 minutes.

》Meanwhile, peel the celeriac and cut into large pieces. Cook for 30 minutes in a saucepan filled with boiling salted water. Drain and blend with a hand blender, adding the butter a little at a time, to form a purée. Season with salt and pepper and keep hot in a double boiler.

》When the pork has cooked for 1 hour 30 minutes, place the figs in the drip tray beneath it. Turn over the pork and cook for a further 30 minutes, then turn the meat a final time and give it a final 30-minute cooking.

》Take the pork out of the oven and rest for 15 minutes, covered with aluminum foil. Carve into thick slices and serve with the figs and the celeriac purée.

PIGS' FEET AND MUSHROOM PATTIES WITH BAY LEAF GRAVY

PREPARATION: **40 minutes**
REFRIGERATION: **30 minutes**
COOKING TIME: **30 minutes**

INGREDIENTS

Serves 6

- 4 cooked pigs' feet
- 9 oz (250 g) oyster mushrooms
- 1 yellow onion
- $^1/_3$ cup (80 g) butter
- 2 tbsp chopped flat-leaf parsley
- 1 cup (80 g) breadcrumbs
- 1 large piece pig's caul
  (or 6 slices of bacon)
- 1¼ cups (300 ml) veal broth
- 4 bay leaves
- 2 tbsp vegetable oil
- salt, freshly ground pepper

》Remove all the bones from the pigs' feet (there are many very small bones). Grind the flesh.

》Clean the mushrooms and chop them coarsely. Peel and chop the onion.

》Heat 2 tablespoons (30 g) of butter in a skillet and cook the onion for 5 minutes over medium heat. Add the mushrooms and season with salt and pepper. Continue cooking over medium heat for 6–8 minutes, stirring frequently, and then add the parsley, breadcrumbs, and ground meat. Stir thoroughly. Transfer to a large bowl and cool.

》Cut the pig's caul into 6 large pieces and spread them out on the work counter. Divide the cold pork mixture into 6 portions and place one in the center of each piece of pig's caul, or slice of bacon. Wrap each portion tightly in its piece of caul (or bacon), so that the ground meat is completely covered. Put the patties on a plate and chill in the freezer for 30 minutes.

》Meanwhile, boil the veal broth in a saucepan with the bay leaves and a pinch each of salt and pepper until reduced by half. Whisk in 1½ tablespoons (20g) of chilled butter. Strain and keep this gravy hot in a double boiler.

》Heat the oil and the remaining butter in a large skillet. When the oil and fat starts to sizzle, place the patties in it and fry for 15 minutes, turning and basting frequently. Drain the patties on absorbent paper towels. Serve immediately with the gravy and a crisp salad.

PORK ROAST WITH CHORIZO AND MANCHEGO CHEESE

PREPARATION: **20 minutes**
COOKING TIME: **1 hour**
STANDING TIME: **15 minutes**

INGREDIENTS

Serves 6

- blade shoulder of pork, boneless, weighing approx. 2¼ lb (1 kg)
- 9 oz (250 g) strongly flavored chorizo sausage
- 9 oz (250 g) Manchego cheese (semisoft Spanish ewe's milk cheese)
- scant 1 tsp chili powder
- 3 tbsp olive oil
- salt

≫ Pre-heat the oven to 340 °F (170 °C).

≫ Remove the skin from the chorizo and slice the sausage into thin rounds. Remove the rind from the Manchego and slice thinly.

≫ Make very deep vertical cuts in the piece of pork about ¾ inch (2 cm) apart—take care not to cut all the way through so that the meat is still attached. Season the cut sections with salt and chili powder and place equal numbers of slices of cheese and sausage between them. Tie the meat and its contents very securely with kitchen twine so that none of the cheese or sausage slices can fall out.

≫ Place the prepared meat in an ovenproof dish and brush all over with olive oil. Roast in the oven for about 1 hour, basting the roast frequently with its own juices.

≫ Take the roast meat out of the oven, wrap in aluminum foil, and rest for 15 minutes.

≫ Carve the pork roast carefully, remove the kitchen twine, and serve immediately.

BRAISED PIGS' CHEEKS WITH STAR ANISE

PREPARATION: **30 minutes**
COOKING TIME: **1½ hours**

INGREDIENTS

Serves 6

- 12 pigs' cheeks
- 1 onion
- ⅓ cup (80 ml) olive oil
- 2½ cups (600 ml) dry white wine
- 1 cup (250 ml) strong veal broth
  (see recipe on page 12)
- 3 star anise
- 1 large bulb fennel
- 3 tbsp heavy cream
- salt, freshly ground pepper

≫ Peel and chop the onion.

≫ Heat 3½ tablespoons (50 ml) of olive oil in a flameproof dish and seal the meat for 5 minutes over high heat, stirring and turning the pigs' cheeks. Add the onion and cook for 3 minutes. Pour in the white wine, bring to a boil, and cook for 5 minutes. Pour in the veal broth and add the star anise. Season with salt and pepper. Simmer gently, covered, over low heat for 1 hour, turning the pigs' cheeks halfway through the cooking time.

≫ Meanwhile, remove the outermost layer of the fennel and cut the bulb into small cubes. Heat the remaining olive oil in a skillet and cook the fennel for 10 minutes over low heat. Season with salt and pepper.

≫ When the pigs' cheeks are done, take them out of the flame-proof dish and reduce the liquid over high heat. Add the cream and reduce for a few more minutes. Whisk the sauce (or use a hand blender) to form an emulsion.

≫ Put the pigs' cheeks back in the sauce and add the fennel. Reheat for a few minutes over low heat before serving.

As an accompaniment, serve a purée of celeriac mixed with butter and a few toasted cumin seeds.

SLOW-COOKED PORK WITH FOUR-SPICE MIX

PREPARATION: 30 minutes
COOKING TIME: 2½ hours
STANDING TIME: 30 minutes

INGREDIENTS

Serves 6

- 1 pork arm shoulder (with bone) weighing about 4½ lb (2 kg)
- 3 large onions
- 2 garlic cloves
- 2 tbsp four-spice mix (ground black peppercorns, nutmeg, cloves, and ginger)
- 3 tbsp olive oil
- 7 tbsp (100 g) jaggery (palm sugar) or brown sugar
- ²/₃ cup (150 ml) white wine vinegar
- salt, freshly ground pepper

〉 Pre-heat the oven to 320 °F (160 °C).

〉 Peel the onions and cut them into quarters. Peel the garlic.

〉 Rub the pork all over by hand with the four-spice mix combined with a little salt and pepper.

〉 Heat the oil in a large flameproof dish and seal the pork over high heat until well browned. Add the onions and the garlic cloves and cook for 5 minutes over low heat. Sprinkle with the sugar and the vinegar and bring to a boil. Pour in 1¼ cups (300 ml) of water, add a little more salt and pepper, and bring to a boil again.

〉 Cover the dish with its lid and place in the oven. Cook for 2 hours 30 minutes, turning the pork every 30 minutes.

〉 Take the dish out of the oven and leave to rest, undisturbed, for 30 minutes before serving.

PORK CHOPS WITH EMMENTAL CHEESE AND HAM STUFFING

PREPARATION: 20 minutes
COOKING TIME: 30 minutes
STANDING TIME: 10 minutes

INGREDIENTS

Serves 6
- 6 thick pork chops
- 6 thin slices dry-cured ham
- generous 1 cup (120 g) grated Emmental cheese
- 7 oz (200 g) pig's caul (or 6 slices of bacon)
- 2½ tbsp (40 g) butter
- 3 tbsp olive oil
- salt, freshly ground pepper

≫ Pre-heat the oven to 340 °F (170 °C).

≫ Rinse the pig's caul then soak it in a large bowl of cold water.

≫ Cut each slice of ham into 3 pieces.

≫ Make a horizontal cut into the pork chops, slicing from the outside towards the bone. Open up this deep pocket in each pork chop and season with salt and pepper. Insert a little Emmental cheese in each of the pockets, place 3 pieces of ham on top of the cheese, and cover with the remaining cheese. Close the pockets, pressing gently.

≫ Drain the pig's caul and squeeze out excess moisture by hand. Spread it out on the work counter and cut into 6 large pieces. Carefully wrap each pork chop in a piece of caul (or, alternatively, a slice of bacon).

≫ Heat the butter and oil in a large skillet over medium heat, add the chops, reduce the heat to low, and fry them for 6–8 minutes on each side to brown them.

≫ Transfer the chops, along with the oil and butter used for frying them, to an ovenproof dish. Cook in the oven for 15 minutes, basting halfway through the cooking time.

≫ Take the dish out of the oven, cover with a sheet of aluminum foil, and rest the chops for 10 minutes before serving.

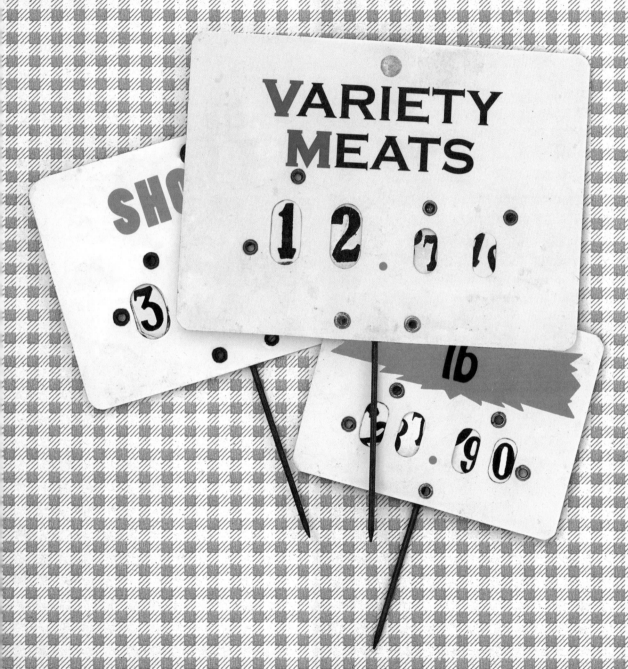

Andouillette skewers with shallot relish

PREPARATION: 45 minutes
COOKING TIME: 30 minutes

INGREDIENTS

Serves 6
- 2¼ lb (1 kg) andouillette (small, cooked, unsmoked sausages made with pork variety meats)
- 14 oz (400 g) shallots
- ⅓ cup (80 g) butter
- ⅔ cup (150 ml) strong veal broth (see recipe on page 12)
- 1¾ lb (750 g) waxy potatoes
- 2 tbsp soft fresh white cheese
- 2 tbsp best-quality mustard
- 2 tbsp mustard seeds
- 1 egg
- 3 tbsp vegetable oil
- salt, freshly ground pepper

》 Cut the andouillette sausages into slices about ¾ inch (2 cm) thick. Thread an equal number of these on to 6 skewers. Put to one side.

》 Peel and slice the shallots. Cook in a flameproof casserole dish with 4 tablespoons (60 g) of butter over low heat for 10 minutes, until very soft. Season with salt and pepper. Pour in the veal broth and simmer for 10 minutes over low heat.

》 Pre-heat the oven to 355 °F (180 °C).

》 While the shallots are cooking, peel the potatoes and grate them into a large bowl. Add the soft white cheese, the mustard, mustard seeds, and the lightly beaten egg. Season with salt and pepper. Stir well.

》 Heat the remaining butter and the oil in a large skillet. Transfer the potato mixture to the skillet and press the potatoes down evenly with the back of a spatula, to form a potato cake. Fry for 5–7 minutes over medium heat and then turn the potato cake by sliding it on to a plate, placing another plate on top, inverting, and sliding the potato cake back into the skillet. Cook the other side for 5–7 minutes.

》 Slide the potato cake carefully onto a baking tray covered with siliconized paper. Place in the oven to finish cooking for 15 minutes.

》 While the potato cake is cooking, broil or grill the andouillette sausage skewers for 6–8 minutes on each side, using a broiler or barbecue. Season with salt and pepper. Serve at once with slices of the potato cake and the shallot relish.

SWEETBREADS WITH GRAPEFRUIT CHUTNEY

PREPARATION: **35 minutes**
STANDING TIME: **overnight**
COOKING TIME: **1¼ hours**

INGREDIENTS

Serves 6
- 2¾ lb (1.2 kg) veal sweetbreads
- 2 large grapefruits
- 1 oz (25 g) fresh ginger, grated
- 3½ tbsp (50 g) granulated sugar
- 3 tbsp rice vinegar
- 3¼ lb (1.5 kg) young parsnips
- 13 tbsp (180 g) butter
- 3 tbsp vegetable oil
- salt, freshly ground pepper

≫ The day before, soak the sweetbreads in a large bowl of cold water for 1 hour. Drain them, transfer to a saucepan, and pour in enough water to cover. Heat to boiling point and simmer very gently for 5 minutes over low heat.

≫ Drain the sweetbreads again and refresh under gently running cold water. Clean them by hand, removing the membranes and small blood vessels. Place them in a strainer with a plate and weight on top and chill overnight in the refrigerator.

≫ The next day, peel the grapefruits down to the juicy flesh and extract the segments from the membranes. Place the segments in a saucepan with the ginger, sugar, and vinegar. Cook gently for 40–45 minutes over low heat to make a chutney.

≫ Meanwhile, peel the parsnips and cut into pieces. Cook in boiling salted water for 30 minutes. Drain and blend (in a food processor or with a hand blender) with 5½ ounces (150 g) of butter, added in small pieces, and a seasoning of salt and pepper, until very smooth. Keep hot in a double boiler.

≫ Blend the grapefruit mixture with a hand blender and cool.

≫ Heat the remaining butter and the oil in a large skillet and as soon as the mixture starts to sizzle, add the sweetbreads. Season with salt and pepper. Fry for a total of 15–20 minutes, turning them frequently and basting with the hot oil and butter. Drain on absorbent paper towels. Serve immediately with the parsnip purée and grapefruit chutney.

BEEF FLANK WITH LEMON GRASS

PREPARATION: **30 minutes**
MARINADE: **6 hours**
COOKING TIME: **20 minutes**

INGREDIENTS

Serves 6

- 6 pieces beef flank weighing approx. 7 oz (200 g) each
- 2 stalks lemon grass
- 7 tbsp (100 ml) soy sauce
- 7 tbsp (100 ml) sweet soy sauce
- 7 tbsp (100 ml) olive oil
- 1 tbsp grated ginger
- 1 tbsp granulated sugar
- 2 green bell peppers
- 2 red bell peppers
- 2 yellow bell peppers
- scant 1 tsp cilantro seeds
- 3 sprigs cilantro
- salt, freshly ground pepper

❯ Remove the outer leaves of the lemon grass stalks and thinly slice the tender inner part.

❯ Use a whisk to mix the two types of soy sauce in a bowl with 2 cups (500 ml) olive oil and the grated ginger, lemon grass, sugar, and a little pepper.

❯ Place the pieces of beef flank in a deep dish. Pour the marinade over the meat to cover it completely. Cover with plastic wrap and chill in the refrigerator for at least 6 hours.

❯ Peel the bell peppers and cut the flesh into short, very narrow strips. Coarsely crush the cilantro seeds. Snip the fresh cilantro into small pieces.

❯ Heat the remaining oil in a skillet and cook the bell pepper strips with the crushed cilantro seeds and a little salt and pepper for 10 minutes over medium heat, stirring frequently. Add the snipped cilantro leaves, cover, and keep hot.

❯ Take the pieces of beef flank out of the marinade. Cook them in a cast-iron griddle on the stove or in a non-stick skillet, with no added oil or butter, for 4–8 minutes, depending on whether you like your meat rare, medium, or well done. Sprinkle the meat with a little of the marinade when it is almost done. Serve immediately, accompanied by the cilantro-flavored bell peppers.

VEAL KIDNEYS WITH RED WINE AND CHERVIL SAUCE

PREPARATION: **30 minutes**
COOKING TIME: **35 minutes**
STANDING TIME: **5 minutes**

INGREDIENTS

Serves 6

- 6 small whole veal kidneys, all fat removed, prepared by your butcher
- 3½ oz (100 g) carrots
- 3½ oz (100 g) onion
- 3½ oz (100 g) celery
- 3¼ cups (750 ml) red wine
- generous 1 tbsp brown unrefined cane sugar (cassonade)
- 7 tbsp (100 ml) strong veal broth (see recipe on page 12)
- 3 large sprigs chervil
- 3½ tbsp (50 g) butter
- 3½ tbsp (50 ml) vegetable oil
- salt, freshly ground pepper

》 Peel and dice the carrots, onion, and celery.

》 Place the diced vegetables in a large saucepan. Pour in the red wine and then add the brown sugar and a pinch each of salt and pepper. Bring to a boil and simmer very gently until the wine has reduced by three-quarters and the liquid has started to thicken. Pour in the veal broth and continue reducing until the sauce has a velvety texture and looks glossy.

》 Pick the chervil leaves off their stalks and coarsely chop them. Strain the sauce into a saucepan. Whisk in 1½ tablespoons (25 g) of chilled butter, cut into small pieces, followed by the chervil. Keep this sauce hot without boiling it.

》 Pre-heat the oven to 390 °F (200 °C).

》 Heat the remaining butter and the oil in a large flameproof dish and seal all the surfaces of the kidneys (left whole) over high heat. Season with salt and pepper. Place the dish in the oven and cook for 8—15 minutes, depending on whether you like your meat rare, medium, or well done. Baste the kidneys with the cooking juices halfway through.

》 Take the kidneys out of the oven, drain on a rack, and rest them, covered with a piece of aluminum foil. Serve with the red wine and chervil sauce, accompanied by fresh tagliatelle.

INDIVIDUAL GRATINS OF OXTAIL AND POTATO

PREPARATION: **50 minutes**
COOKING TIME: **4 hours**

INGREDIENTS

Serves 6
- 3¼ lb (1.5 kg) oxtail, cut into
  sections
- 1 carrot
- 1 onion
- 1 stick celery
- 3 tbsp olive oil
- 2½ cups (600 ml) dry red wine
- 1²/₃ cups (400 ml) veal broth
- 1¾ lb (800 g) celeriac
- 1 very large floury potato
- 2 sprigs sage
- 7 tbsp (100 g) butter
- 3½ oz (100 g) breadcrumbs
- salt, freshly ground pepper

❯ Peel and dice the carrot, onion, and celery. Heat the olive oil in a large flameproof dish and seal the pieces of oxtail over high heat. Pour in the wine and boil for 5 minutes. Add the diced vegetables and the veal broth. Season with salt and pepper. Simmer gently, covered, for 3 hours over low heat, skimming the surface frequently—when fully cooked the meat should come off the bone easily. Cool in the cooking liquid.

❯ While the oxtail is cooking, peel the celeriac and the potato and cut into pieces. Cook the celeriac and potato together for 20 minutes over medium heat in a large saucepan filled with boiling water to which you have added salt and pepper.

≫ Pick the leaves from the sage sprigs and chop finely.

≫ Drain the celeriac and the potato and reduce to a purée with a hand blender, adding ⅓ cup (80 g) of butter along with half the sage.

≫ Pre-heat the oven to 355 °F (180 °C). Lift the pieces of oxtail out of the liquid and take all the meat off the bones. Place the meat in a large bowl.

≫ Strain generous ¾ cup (200 ml) of the cooking liquid into a flameproof dish and boil to reduce by half. Stir in the meat with the remaining sage and a little more salt and pepper, if desired.

≫ Spoon equal amounts of the meat mixture into 6 fairly small, deep, individual ovenproof dishes and cover with the celeriac and potato purée. Sprinkle the surface with bread crumbs and dot with butter. Heat in the oven for 20–30 minutes—the tops should brown—and serve immediately. (You can prepare this recipe in advance and reheat and brown the individual gratins of oxtail and potato shortly before serving.)

CABBAGE PARCELS STUFFED WITH BEEF CHEEK

PREPARATION: 50 minutes
COOKING TIME: 3¾ hours

INGREDIENTS

Serves 6

- 2¾ lb (1.2 kg) beef cheek, trimmed and trussed
- 3 tbsp vegetable oil
- 2 sticks celery, peeled and diced
- 2 carrots, peeled and diced
- 1 onion, peeled and diced
- 2 cloves garlic, peeled and fine diced
- 5 cups (1.2 litres) dry red wine
- 1¼ cups (300 ml) veal broth
- 2 tomatoes, cut into pieces
- 1 bouquet garni
- 1 Savoy cabbage
- salt, freshly ground pepper

》 Heat the oil in a flameproof dish and brown the meat on all sides over high heat. Transfer the piece of beef to a plate.

》 Add the vegetables to the oil left in the dish and cook for 2 minutes over medium heat. Add the wine, season with salt and pepper, and bring to a boil. Replace the meat in the dish. Add the veal broth, the tomatoes, and the bouquet garni. Simmer gently, covered, for 3½ hours over low heat, skimming the surface frequently. Cool the meat in the cooking liquid.

》 Remove and discard the outermost leaves of the cabbage and select 6 undamaged, crisp large leaves. Blanch these for 4–5 minutes in a large saucepan filled with boiling salted water. Drain the leaves and refresh them by plunging them into a bowl of cold water.

》 Take the beef cheek carefully out of its cooking liquid, remove the trussing twine, and break up the meat into small shreds in a large bowl.

》 Reduce the cooking liquid until it is fairly thick and glossy. Moisten the meat with a little of this liquid.

》 Place a portion of meat in the center of each cabbage leaf and wrap the leaf around tightly to enclose it. Wrap the stuffed cabbage leaves with plastic wrap to secure.

》 Strain the remaining cooking liquid into a double boiler. Adjust the seasoning (1 tablespoon of sugar can be added at this point to sweeten the sauce). Keep very hot.

》 Shortly before serving the stuffed cabbage leaves, reheat them by steaming them in a bamboo or regular steamer. After reheating, carefully remove the plastic wrap using scissors and serve with the sauce.

CRUNCHY SLICES OF ROLLED CALF'S HEAD AND TONGUE WITH CAPERS

PREPARATION: 40 minutes
STANDING TIME: overnight
COOKING TIME: 4 hours

INGREDIENTS

Serves 6
- 3¼ lb (1.5 kg) piece rolled and tied calf's head and tongue, prepared by your butcher
- 2 onions, peeled
- 2 cloves
- 2 carrots, peeled
- 2 sticks celery, peeled
- 1 bouquet garni
- 3 hard-cooked eggs
- 3½ oz (100 g) capers
- 1 bunch parsley
- 1 tsp mustard
- 3 tbsp cider vinegar
- 3 tbsp sunflower oil
- 3 tbsp walnut oil
- salt, freshly ground pepper

≫ Stud 1 onion with the cloves.

≫ Place the meat in a kettle or stockpot and cover with cold water. Bring to a boil and boil over medium heat for 5 minutes. Drain and rinse the meat under running cold water.

≫ Clean the cooking vessel and return the meat to it along with the vegetables , salt, and pepper. Cover with cold water and bring to a boil. Place a heavy, heatproof plate on top of the meat to keep it submerged, cover, and simmer gently over low heat for 3 hours 30 minutes—3 hours 45 minutes (when cooked the blade of a knife should slide easily into the meat). Cool the meat in the cooking liquid. When cold, drain, wrap in aluminum foil, and chill overnight in the refrigerator.

≫ Shortly before serving, chop the hard-cooked eggs with a knife. Drain and chop the capers. Rinse and chop the parsley. Mix the eggs in a large bowl with the capers, parsley, mustard, vinegar, and oil. Season with salt and pepper to taste.

≫ Pre-heat the oven to 300 °F (150 °C). Cut the rolled calf's head and tongue into 6 very large, thick slices.

≫ Pre-heat a very wide non-stick skillet for a short time with no added oil or fat and place the meat slices in it, 1 or 2 at a time. Dry-fry for 6–8 minutes on each side to ensure that both sides are crunchy and golden-brown. Transfer to a very large serving platter lined with a sheet of siliconized paper. Place in the oven, uncovered, for 10 minutes.

≫ Serve with the caper sauce. A green salad and steamed potatoes go well with this dish.

Hanger steaks (beef onglets) with onion and date relish

PREPARATION: 20 minutes
COOKING TIME: 50 minutes

INGREDIENTS

Serves 6

- 6 beef hanger steaks (onglets) weighing approx. 7 oz (200g) each
- 1 bunch small white onions or scallions
- 6 large soft, fleshy dates
- 4 tbsp (60 g) butter
- 3 tbsp white wine vinegar
- 4½ tbsp (60 g) granulated sugar
- generous 2 tbsp mustard seeds
- salt, freshly ground pepper

≫ Peel the onions, leaving a little of their green stalk attached, and cut into thick slices.

≫ Pit the dates (if not already pitted) and cut into small pieces.

≫ Melt the butter in a flameproof dish and cook the onions in it for 10 minutes over medium heat. Add the dates, vinegar, and sugar. Season with salt and pepper. Cook for 15 minutes over low heat so the ingredients soften and combine.

≫ Stir in the mustard seeds (and 3 tablespoons of water if the mixture is too thick). Cook for a further 15 minutes over low heat, when the onions should have almost disintegrated.

≫ Just before you plan to serve the steaks, pre-heat a cast-iron griddle (or cook on a barbecue) and cook for 4–8 minutes on each side, depending on whether you like your meat rare, medium, or well done. Season with salt and pepper.

≫ Serve the steaks with the onion and date relish and best-quality mild mustard.

CONVERSIONS

LIQUIDS

Metric	American measure	Imperial
5 ml	1 tsp	1 tsp
15 ml	1 tbsp	1 tbsp
35 ml	2½ tbsp	2½ tbsp
65 ml	¼ cup	2 fl oz
125 ml	½ cup	4½ fl oz
250 ml	1 cup	9 fl oz
500 ml	2 cups	17 fl oz
1 liter	4 cups	1 quart

SOLIDS

Metric	American measure	Imperial
30 g	1 oz	1 oz
55 g	2 oz	2 oz
115 g	4 oz	4 oz
170 g	6 oz	6 oz
225 g	8 oz	8 oz
454 g	1 lb	1 lb

OVEN TEMPERATURES

Temperature	° Celsius	° Fahrenheit	Gas mark
Very cool	140 °C	275 °F	1
Cool	150 °C	300 °F	2
Warm	160 °C	325 °F	3
Moderate	180 °C	350 °F	4
Fairly hot	190–200 °C	375–400 °F	5–6
Hot	220 °C	425 °F	7
Very hot	230–240 °C	450–475 °F	8–9

A big thank you to
Barbara and Aurélie for their confidence in this project.
Pierre-Louis for his beautiful photographs.
Yves-Charles and his magnificent knives (www.couteau.com)
Staub, Le Creuset, and Mauviel for their dishes.

It is advisable not to serve dishes that contain raw eggs to
very young children, pregnant women, elderly people, or to
anyone weakened by serious illness. If in any doubt, consult
your doctor. Be sure that all the eggs you use are as fresh as
possible.

© Mango, Paris — 2013
Original Title: *Boucherie ! Recettes de Viandes à Partager*
ISBN 978-23-17001-30-7

Editorial Director: Barbara Sabatier
Editor: Aurélie Cazenave
Graphic Design: Laurent Quellet and Astrid de Lassée
Photoengraving: A4
Production: Thierry Dubus and Marie Guibert

© for this English edition: h.f. ullmann publishing GmbH

Translation from French: Anna Bennett and Sara Harris in
association with First Edition Translations Ltd, Cambridge, UK

Project management for h.f. ullmann publishing:
Katharina Pferdmenges, Isabel Weiler

Overall responsibility for production: h.f. ullmann publishing
GmbH, Potsdam, Germany

Printed in India, 2015

ISBN 978-3-8480-0756-1

10 9 8 7 6 5 4 3 2 1
X IX VIII VII VI V IV III II I

www.ullmann-publishing.com
newsletter@ullmann-publishing.com
facebook.com/ullmann.social